Sarah A.

THE PERSONAL LIFE OF QUEEN VICTORIA

ARCADIA PRESS

Copyright © Sarah A. Tooley

*The Personal Life of
Queen Victoria*
(1897)

Arcadia Press 2018

www.arcadiapress.eu
info@arcadiapress.eu

TABLE OF CONTENTS

PREFACE..7

THE CHILDHOOD OF QUEEN VICTORIA..9

THE GIRLHOOD OF QUEEN VICTORIA...22

THE MAIDEN MONARCH..36

BETROTHAL AND EARLY MARRIED LIFE OF QUEEN VICTORIA...........49

HOME AND COURT LIFE OF QUEEN VICTORIA...................................63

THE LATER MARRIED LIFE OF QUEEN VICTORIA...............................75

THE WIDOWED MONARCH..88

VICTORIA, QUEEN AND EMPRESS...98

PERSONAL TASTES AND CHARACTERISTICS OF QUEEN VICTORIA. .110

THE PERSONAL LIFE OF QUEEN VICTORIA

PREFACE

THE aim of the writer of this "Life" has been to narrate those incidents which tend most to reveal the personal history and character of the Queen, and no attempt has been made to deal with the events of her reign which belong more to the historian than to the personal biographer. In writing of one so illustrious and far removed from ordinary acquaintance and observation, the difficulties of faithful portraiture are apparent; but the frank manner in which Her Majesty has revealed the details of her domestic life in Sir Theodore Martin's "Life of the Prince Consort," the two volumes of "Leaves from Our Journal in the Highlands," and the "Memoir of Princess Alice," makes the task easier. In addition to these sources of information, I am indebted to the "Greville Memoirs," the "Life of Baron Stockmar," Lady Bloomfield's "Reminiscences," the Bunsen and Malmesbury "Memoirs," and many other "Lives" and "Reminiscences" of eminent courtiers and statesmen which throw side lights upon the Queen's private life. Among the many books written upon Her Majesty, I have found none more suggestive than the biographies by Jefferson, Barnett Smith, and Grace Greenwood, and Humphrey's "Queen at Balmoral." Fugitive literature throughout the reign has been laid under contribution as affording pictures of scenes and events as they passed before the public eye.

A large amount of private information has been kindly given by those personally acquainted with Her Majesty, and who have had the opportunity for observing the attractiveness and dignity of her character in private; and to them I am indebted for many of the incidents and anecdotes related. Canon Davys, son of the Queen's tutor, a former Bishop of Peterborough, has also supplied much interesting information regarding her early years.

SARAH A. TOOLEY.

THE CHILDHOOD OF QUEEN VICTORIA

AN American gentleman being called upon, at a banquet in London, to propose the health of Her Gracious Majesty the Queen, did so in the following terms: "The Queen of England, the Empress of India, the Woman of the world." Nothing could more happily have expressed the keynote to the love and loyalty which have surrounded the throne of Victoria — it is her womanliness which has held the heart of the nation. The laws of heredity and of environment make no distinction between king and peasant; and it is to the parentage and early training of the Queen that we must look to see how her character, so distinguished by womanly virtues and domestic graces, has been moulded.

We find that her father, the Duke of Kent, fourth son of George III., was deservedly known as the "Popular Duke." He was a tall, stately man of soldierly bearing, characterised by courteous and engaging manners, and was generous to a fault. He was connected with no less than sixty-five charitable organisations at the time of his death. From him the Queen has inherited her love of order and punctuality, and she is fond of referring to his connection with the Army. Once, when presenting new colours to the Royal Scots, she said to the men: "I have been associated with your regiment from my earliest infancy, as my dear father was your Colonel. He was proud of his profession, and I was always taught to consider myself a soldier's child." Fit complement to the soldier-Duke was the Queen's mother, who, without being a beauty, was a charming and attractive woman, elegant in figure, with fine brown eyes and luxuriant brown hair. She was warmly affectionate, free and gracious in her manner, but withal a duchess of duchesses to her fingertips, as after events showed. Above everything else, she was distinguished for motherly devotion and the domestic virtues. It was these characteristics which caused the Duke of Kent to fall in love with her. He was entrusted in 1818, by Prince Leopold of Saxe-Coburg, then in retirement at Claremont mourning his young wife, the beloved Princess Charlotte, with letters to his sister, the Princess of Leiningen, who was a young widow living a retired life in her castle at

Amorbach, Bavaria, superintending the education of her two children. The Duke of Kent, a bachelor of fifty, was entirely charmed by the picture of domestic felicity which he found when he arrived at Castle Amorbach, and in due time became the affianced husband of the widowed Princess.

They were married at Coburg on the 29th of May, 1818, according to the rites of the Lutheran Church, and re-married in England shortly afterwards at a private ceremony at Kew Palace, after which they returned to Bavaria. The prospect of the birth of a child, however, made the Duke of Kent anxious to bring his wife to England, so that his coming heir might be "Briton-born." He thought at first of taking a house in Lanarkshire, in which case the Queen would have been born a Scotchwoman; but he finally decided on a suite of rooms at Kensington Palace. Brave indeed was the Duchess of Kent to quit her native land and her kindred to undertake a tedious journey by land and sea within a short time of her confinement. So solicitous was the Duke for her safety that throughout the whole of the journey by land he suffered no one to drive her but himself. The Duchess reached Kensington Palace in safety, and at four o'clock on the morning of the 24th of May, 1819, a pretty little princess was born, who, according to Baron Stockmar, was as "plump as a partridge."

One may be permitted to say that the Duke was ridiculously proud of his wee girlie, and is said to have cried for joy when she was presented to the royal and official persons who had been awaiting news of her birth in the ante-chamber. Although several lives stood between the infant Princess and the throne, her father had a prophetic instinct that she was destined to be Queen of England. "Take care of her," he would say; "she may yet be Queen of England." No disappointment was ever expressed that the child was a girl. The grief which had filled the country when the Princess Charlotte died showed that the people were eager for a queen, a sentiment referred to by the Dowager Duchess of Coburg when writing congratulations to her daughter, the Duchess of Kent. "Again a Charlotte," she writes, "destined perhaps to play a great part one day, if a brother is not born to take it out of her hands. The English like queens, and the niece of the ever-lamented, beloved Princess Charlotte will be most dear to them." It was Grandmamma of Coburg who named the new-comer the blossom of May. "How pretty the little Mayflower will be," she writes, "when I see it in a year's time! Siebold [the nurse] cannot sufficiently describe what a dear little love it is." Siebold was a lady doctor from Berlin, popularly known as "Dr. Charlotte," who attended the Duchess of Kent at her confinement, she having declined the services of the male physicians in attendance at the Palace. Three months later Dr. Charlotte returned to Germany to officiate at the birth of a little prince, one day to be the husband of his pretty cousin the "Mayflower," who was merrily crowing in the old palace of Kensington. When the children were in their cradles, that charming and vivacious old lady, Grandmamma of Coburg, with matchmaking propensity, wrote of little Prince Albert, "What a charming pendant he would be to the pretty cousin!" Unfortunately she was not spared to see the day when her fondest wish was realised by the marriage of her grandson with her granddaughter, the "Mayflower," who had blossomed into a sweet young queen.

Nothing could have been more propitious than the birth of our beloved Queen. She was a thrice-welcome child, born of a happy union between parents distinguished for goodness and piety, and from the hour of her birth she basked in the sunshine of love. She came when the world of nature was fresh and jubilant — the sweet spring-time, when birds were singing, trees budding, and the air fragrant with the odour of flowers. Small wonder that she was a lovely baby. She had flaxen hair, blue eyes, a fair skin, and was the picture of health — chubby, rosy, beautifully formed, and of a happy, lively disposition. The Duchess of Kent nursed her at her own breast, and in the absence of the Princess's special nurse, Mrs. Brock, dressed and undressed the little one herself. Robert Owen, the Socialist, is said to have been the first man who held the Princess in his arms, he having called to see the Duke of Kent on business shortly after her arrival. The christening of the infant Princess took place in the Grand Saloon of Kensington Palace, the gold font from the Tower being brought for the occasion. The Archbishop of Canterbury and the Bishop of London officiated. The sponsors were the Prince Regent in person, the Emperor Alexander of Russia, represented by the Duke of York, the Queen-Dowager of Wurtemberg, represented by the Princess Augusta, and the Dowager Duchess of Coburg, represented by the Dowager Duchess of Gloucester. The Duke of Kent was anxious that his "little Queen" should be named Elizabeth, but the Prince Regent gave the name Alexandrina, after the Emperor of Russia, upon which the Duke asked that another name might be associated with it; then the Prince Regent, who according to Greville was annoyed that the infant was not to be named Georgiana, after himself, said, "Give her her mother's name also." Accordingly the Princess was named Alexandrina Victoria. For a while she was called Princess Alexandrina or "little Drina"; but gradually her mother's name prevailed, and she was known only as the Princess Victoria. This choice was confirmed by the Queen herself when she signed her first State document simply Victoria. Shortly after the christening the Duchess of Kent was publicly "churched" at St. Mary Abbott's, Kensington, the Duke himself conducting her with much ceremony to the communion table.

The first eight months of the Queen's life were passed at Kensington Palace, where glimpses of her, laughing and crowing at her nursery window, were often caught by strollers through the Gardens. The Duke was always pleased to have her shown to the people, and when she was only four months old took her in the carriage with him to a review on Hounslow Heath. The Prince Regent, annoyed at the attention which she created, sharply remonstrated, saying, "That infant is too young to be brought into public." At three months old the Princess was vaccinated, and was the first royal baby to be inoculated after the method of Jenner.

In order to escape the rigour of the winter, the Duke and Duchess removed, at the end of the year, with their darling child, into Devonshire, staying at Woolbrook Glen, Sidmouth, a lovely retreat lying back from the sea, and surrounded by picturesque grounds. On their way to Sidmouth the royal party stayed two days with the Bishop of Salisbury. His Lordship was fond of jumping the little Princess in his arms, and during one of these frolics she seized hold of the good man's wig and shook it so violently with her dimpled hands that she covered herself with powder, and was not prevailed upon to loosen her clutches until she had pulled off a tuft of hair also.

I have found no more charming glimpse of this period of the Queen's infancy than is recorded by Mrs. Marshall in her "Recollections of Althea Allingham." The Allinghams were living at Sidmouth at the time of the royal visit, and we get this graphic picture of the local interest it elicited.

"'I have just heard a piece of news,' Oliffe said. 'The Duke of Kent has taken the "Glen" at the farther end of the village, and the servants are expected to-morrow to put the place in order for the Duke and Duchess of Kent and the little Princess Victoria.'" Sidmouth was elated at the prospect of receiving the royal party, and Mrs. Allingham's little daughters were full of anxiety to see the baby Princess. Their expectations were soon realised, and they frequently saw her being taken out for her daily airing. Mrs. Allingham thus describes her: "She was a very fair and lovely baby, and there was, even in her infant days, a charm about her which has never left our gracious Queen. The clear, frank glance of her large blue eyes, and the sweet but firm expression of her mouth, were really remarkable, even when a baby of eight months old."

One bright January morning the Allinghams were returning from an excursion, when they met the Duke and Duchess of Kent, "linked arm in arm," the nurse carrying the little Princess, who looked lovely in a white swansdown hood and pelisse, and was holding out her hand to her father. He took her in his arms as the party drew up in line, respectfully waiting, uncovered and curtseying.

"Stella exclaimed: 'What a beautiful baby!'

"The Duchess hearing, smiled and said, 'Would you like to kiss the baby?'

"Stella coloured with delight, and looked at me [Mrs. Allingham] for permission.

"The Duke kindly held the little Princess down towards Stella, and said:

"'I am glad my little May blossom finds favour in your eyes.'

"Then a shout was heard from the donkey where Stephen sat.

"'Me too, please, Duke.'

"Instead of being in the least shocked with my boy's freedom, the Duke laughed, saying:

"'Dismount, then.'

"Stephen scrambled down, and coming up received the longed-for kiss.

"'Father calls Stella and Benvenuta his May blossoms,' Stephen volunteered.

"'And you may be proud of them,' the Duke said, as he gave the Princess back into her nurse's arms; and the Duchess, with repeated bows and smiles, passed on."

This tender picture of domestic felicity was, alas! soon to be marred by death. The Duke of Kent, returning from an excursion in the vicinity of Sidmouth, sat down in wet boots to play with his little daughter, and was so enchanted with her baby ways that he could not tear himself away to make the needed change of his damp garments. A chill ensued, which resulted in a fatal attack of inflammation of the lungs. He died on the 23rd of January, 1820. Two days later, the good people of Sidmouth, who had welcomed the Duke with so much joy, stood sorrowfully to watch the departure of his widowed Duchess and her babe for London. The little Princess was held up to the carriage window to bid the people farewell, and she sported and laughed joyously, patting the glass with her pretty dimpled hands, in happy unconsciousness of her melancholy loss. Prince Leopold (afterwards King of the Belgians) acted as their escort, he having arrived at Sidmouth just in time to see his sister's husband breathe his last. In his "Reminiscences" he says: "The Duchess, who had lost a most amiable and devoted husband, was in a state of the greatest distress. The poor Duke had left his family deprived of all means of subsistence. The journey to Kensington was very painful, and the weather very severe." From this time forward we find Prince Leopold acting as a father and guardian to his little niece, Victoria. It was he who generously supplemented the jointure of £6,000 which the Duchess of Kent received from the country, and enabled her to rear our future Queen in a manner befitting her position. By her second marriage the Duchess had sacrificed her dowry, and she conscientiously yielded the Duke of Kent's estate to his creditors, so that all that remained to her was her jointure.

The same day on which the Duchess and her infant returned to Kensington, George III. died, and was succeeded by the Prince Regent.

This event, coupled with her father's death, placed the Princess two lives nearer to the throne. The Duchess, doubtless actuated by these circumstances, determined to rear her child in the land over which she might eventually rule, and gave up her own natural desire to return to Bavaria. Speaking of herself and infant at this time, she says: "We stood alone — almost friendless and alone in this country; I could not even speak the language of it. I did not hesitate how to act; I gave up my home, my kindred, my duties [the regency of Leiningen] to devote myself to that duty which was to be the whole object of my future life." Thus nobly did the Duchess of Kent start upon her important work — no light task — the training of a queen. From that day forward she lived at Kensington in stately seclusion, watching over the young "hope of England," who was never allowed to be an hour out of her sight. From the day of her father's death until she ascended the throne, the Queen had never passed a night outside her mother's bedchamber. She had never been seen in public or even heard of except in conjunction with her mother.

The apartments occupied by the Duchess of Kent and the Princess Victoria were in the south-east portions of the Palace, beneath the King's gallery. They are now unused; but a visitor will find in one of the rooms on the principal floor, having three windows looking eastward over Kensington Gardens, a gilt plate upon the wall, with this inscription:

IN THIS ROOM
QUEEN VICTORIA
WAS BORN,
May 24, 1819

A room on the top floor served as the Princess's nursery, and in one corner still stands a doll's house, a headless horse, and the model of a ship, remnants of the toys which delighted her rather monotonous childhood.

Here, in the old Palace which in days gone by had been the stately abode of kings and queens and the scene of gay court revels, the Princess was nurtured in all that was simple, loving, and pure. She had a natural home life free from the formalities of a court. The one misfortune was that she had no companions of her own age:

"For her there was no mate,
A royal child of power and state."

Her step-sister, the Princess Feodore (daughter of the Duchess of Kent by her first marriage), was eleven years her senior, and though the little Princess was devotedly attached to her as an elder sister, she was no playmate for her. A pretty story is told of the visit of the infant harp-player, Lyra, to Kensington Palace, and how delighted the Princess Victoria was — not with the harp-playing, but with having a little girl of her own age to speak to. When the Duchess of Kent returned to the room after a brief absence, she found the two children sitting on the hearthrug with toys strewn around them, enjoying themselves hugely as they laughed and prattled, oblivious of the harp standing desolate, as the one which "rang through Tara's halls." The little Princess dearly loved a romp, as is testified by William Wilberforce, who lived at Gore House, Kensington, and was occasionally received by the Duchess of Kent. The philanthropist, in writing to his friend, Hannah More, says: "In consequence of a very civil message from the Duchess of Kent, I waited on her this morning, and found her with her fine, animated child on the floor by her side with its playthings, of which I soon became one."

The Princess was brought up in the most simple and regular style of living, her whole surroundings being utterly devoid of the pomp and show of royalty. In this early training we find the foundations of that love of simplicity and frugality which has always distinguished our gracious Queen. We well remember being in a country town when the Queen came to unveil a statue of the Prince Consort. The local authorities had provided a sumptuous luncheon, with all the delicacies of the season; but great was the consternation when Her Majesty asked for rice pudding. No such homely dish was included in the menu.

The little Princess's day was passed in the following manner. She rose early, and breakfasted at eight o'clock in the pretty morning-room of the Palace, sitting beside her mother in a little rosewood chair, a table to match in front of her on which was placed her bread and milk and fruit, her nurse standing beside her. After breakfast her half-sister, the Princess Feodore, retired with her governess, Fraulein Lehzen, to study, and the little Victoria mounted her donkey, a present from her uncle, the Duke of York, and rode round Kensington Gardens. From ten to twelve she received instruction from her mother, assisted by Fraulein Lehzen; then came a good romp through the long suite of rooms with her nurse, Mrs. Brock, whom she affectionately called her "dear, dear Boppy." At two o'clock she dined plainly at her mother's luncheon table, afterwards came lessons again until four o'clock, then she went with her mother for a drive, or, if the weather was hot, spent the afternoon in the Gardens under the trees, coming out early in the evening for a turn in her little pony-chaise. The Duchess dined at seven o'clock, at which time the Princess supped at the same table on bread and milk; she then retired for a little play in a farther part of the room along with "dear Boppy," joining her mother again at dessert. At nine o'clock she went to her little French bed with its pretty Chintz hangings, placed beside that of her mother. An occasional visit to Windsor to see her "Uncle King," as she called His Majesty George IV., a sojourn at Claremont with her adored Uncle Leopold, and a few weeks at the sea in autumn, were the only breaks in her little life.

On her fourth birthday she had a great excitement, no less than being bidden by "Uncle King" to attend a State dinner party with her mother at Carlton House. She was dressed for the occasion in a simple white frock looped up on the left sleeve by a miniature of the King, set in diamonds, His Majesty's birthday present to his little niece, whose vivacious manners seemed to have delighted him vastly.

Several stories are told of the quick repartee which "Uncle King" received from his amusing little niece of Kent. During one of her visits to Windsor, the King said, "Now, Victoria, the band is waiting to play; what tune would you like to hear best?"

"'God Save the King,' if you please, uncle," she promptly replied.

And again, when asked what part of her visit had been the greatest treat, she discreetly said, "Oh, the ride in the carriage with you, uncle." On this occasion the King had driven her himself, which was doubtless a great event. We get a further glimpse into these little trips to Windsor in one of Grandmamma Coburg's charming letters. Writing in 1826 to the Duchess of Kent, she says: "I see by the English newspapers that 'His Majesty George IV. and H.R.H. the Duchess of Kent went on Virginia Water.' The little monkey [Princess Victoria] must have pleased and amused him. She is such a pretty, clever child."

A few years later "Uncle King" gave a child's ball in honour of the visit of Donna Maria, the little Queen of Portugal, to this country. This was the first Court ceremonial at which the Princess Victoria was present. A lady of the Court, however, gave great offence to the King by saying how "pretty it would be to see the two little Queens dancing together." His Majesty had no mind as yet to hear his niece of Kent dubbed a queen. By all accounts the juvenile ball was a pretty and brilliant affair. The children of the highest nobility were there, and paid mimic court to the little Queen of Portugal, who sat by the side of the King, dressed in a red velvet frock and literally blazing with jewels from head to foot. This was the first occasion upon which that spicy Court chronicler, Mr. Greville, saw the Princess Victoria; but he appears to have been carried off his head by the dark-eyed Donna of Portugal's brilliant appearance. "Our little Princess," he writes, "is a short, plain-looking child, and not near so good-looking as the Portuguese." Fie upon you, Mr. Greville; did not the fine Donna Maria awkwardly trip in the dance and fall down and bruise her face, while our fair-haired, blue-eyed Princess, in her simple white frock, kept her head and her heels, and was admired by all people of good taste for her natural, unadorned beauty?

Visits to Uncle King were very rare events, as the Duchess of Kent did not wish her little daughter to see much of Court life; but she took her frequently to see her Uncle Leopold at Claremont, and these visits were the most delightful holidays of all. Writing in after years from Claremont to her uncle, then King of the Belgians, the Queen says: "This place brings back recollections of the happiest days of my otherwise dull childhood — days in which I experienced such kindness from you, dearest uncle. Victoria [the Princess Royal] plays with my old bricks, and I see her running and jumping in the flower garden, as old (though I still feel little) Victoria of former days used to do."

In the autumn of 1824, Grandmamma of Coburg was a visitor at Claremont, along with the Duchess of Kent and the Princess Victoria; and it has often been said that she brought her little grandson Prince Albert of Coburg with her, but we believe that this was not the fact. We are fortunate in finding a charming account of the royal party in the letters of Miss Jane Porter, author of "The Scottish Chiefs." She dwelt with her mother and sister in a cottage close to the grounds of Claremont, and had frequent opportunities for seeing the Princess, who, she was delighted to find, resembled her lamented aunt, the Princess Charlotte. Miss Porter describes her as "a beautiful child, with a cherubic form of features, clustered round by glossy fair ringlets. Her complexion was remarkably transparent, with a soft and often heightening tinge of the sweet blush-rose upon her cheeks, that imparted a peculiar brilliancy to her clear blue eyes. Whenever she met any strangers in her usual paths, she always seemed, by the quickness of her glance, to inquire who and what they were."

At home the Princess was not allowed to attend public worship at Kensington Church for fear of attracting too much attention, service being conducted in the Palace by the Duchess herself during her daughter's earliest years, and afterwards by the Rev. George Davys, her tutor. But while at Claremont she was taken to the little village church at Esher. Fortunate Miss Porter had a seat facing the Claremont pew, and we fear that her devotions were somewhat disturbed by the attention which she gave to the movements of the royal visitors, although she is able, at least on one occasion, to give a very good reason for her attentive scrutiny. "I should not voluntarily have so employed myself in church," she piously writes, "but I had seen a wasp skimming backwards and forwards over the head and before the unveiled summer bonnet of the little Princess; and I could not forbear watching the dangerous insect, fearing it might sting her face. She, totally unobserving it, had meanwhile fixed her eyes on the clergyman, who had taken his seat in the pulpit to preach the sermon, and she never withdrew them thence for a moment during his whole discourse." Next day, from a lady personally intimate at Claremont, Miss Porter learned the reason why the Princess riveted her eyes upon the clergyman, who, according to her account, was not an attractive person, so that she saw not the "dangerous insect" — she was required to give her mother not only the text, but the leading heads of the discourse. Poor little Princess! those were the days of long and formal sermons.

It was in the autumn succeeding this visit to Claremont that the Princess paid the first of her many visits to Ramsgate. Three years before she had taken her first sight of the sea at Brighton. During her seaside visits she was allowed to play with other children on the sands, have donkey rides ad libitum, and to run out to meet the on-coming waves. If they chanced to ripple over her little feet, she was in a high state of glee. Then at Ramsgate she used frequently to go to a delightful old dairy-woman's cottage to have a glass of milk before breakfast. We find a graphic sketch of the Princess at this time by a writer in Fraser's Magazine, who in somewhat florid style thus relates his observations: "When first I saw the pale and pretty daughter of the Duke of Kent, she was fatherless. Her fair, light form was sporting in all the redolence of youth and health on the noble sands of old Ramsgate. She wore a plain straw bonnet with a white ribbon round it, and as pretty a pair of shoes on as pretty a pair of feet as I ever remember to have seen from China to Kamschatka. I defy you all to find me a prettier pair of feet than those of the belle Victoria, when she played with the pebbles and the tides on Ramsgate sands." The Princess on this occasion was accompanied by her mother and by William Wilberforce; the latter is said to have beguiled the adventurous Victoria from sporting too freely with the waves by telling her stories of the slave children whom he was labouring to emancipate. As he did so, he stood on the shore, an impressive figure, clasping in his own the tiny hands of the five-years-old Princess, into whose heart his words were sinking deep and were destined to bear glorious fruit in after years. When they turned homeward from the shore down the High Street, the Princess espied an old Irishwoman sitting pale and dejected by the wayside, and literally "teased" a silver coin from her mother to give to this lonely wayfarer.

The Duchess and her daughter frequently returned to visit Ramsgate, staying principally at Townley House, close to the picturesque grounds of East Cliff, the residence of Mr. Moses Montefiore, who courteously provided them with a special key to his private gate in order that they might use his grounds at their pleasure. On the occasion of the Queen's visit to the City of London soon after her accession, Mr. Montefiore received her in his capacity of Sheriff, and one can imagine that Her Majesty was not unmindful of those pleasant days at Ramsgate when she bade him rise up Sir Moses Montefiore. He was the first Jew to receive the honour of knighthood.

But a truce to the little Princess's holiday jaunts; we must continue the thread of her life at Kensington. An old lady friend has often described to me how she used to watch the Princess taking her walks and rides in Kensington Gardens. She never wore smart things, but was plainly and prettily dressed in a straw hat with a ribbon round it — sometimes the hat was lined with blue — and her summer dresses were of simple white cotton, relieved by a coloured silk fichu. She was often to be encountered in the Gardens skipping along between her mother and the Princess Feodore, each of whom held one of her hands. The little one would bow and smile at the passers-by, and say "lady" and "good morning" in a pretty, silvery voice, sometimes holding out her dimpled little hand to be kissed. The wise mother taught her to approach strangers fearlessly, and to return their salutations graciously. Everybody in the neighbourhood grew to love the winsome little Princess. But the prettiest sight of all was to see her mounted on her white donkey, gaily caparisoned with blue ribbons, an old soldier, a former retainer of her father's, leading her bridle rein, while some of the ladies of the household walked by her side. She was then at the height of enjoyment, and, once mounted, "not all the king's horses nor all the king's men" could persuade her to come down again. Her mother had made a little rule that she should ride and walk alternately; but there were not a few scenes, and we fear some screams, in Kensington Gardens when nurse or governess tried to force the little lady to dismount, for she was as wilful as she was engaging. It was only when the old soldier, who was a special favourite, held out his arms for her that she was persuaded to quit her dear donkey's back.

She used sometimes to ride in a pony-chaise over the gravel walks, led by a page. One day a dog ran between the pony's legs, causing the tiny carriage to upset, and the Princess would undoubtedly have been killed by the fall had not a soldier passing at the time caught her clothes and swung her into his arms. His name was Maloney, and he was of course thanked and rewarded by the Duchess of Kent. This was the second providential escape from death which the Queen had in her childhood. The first was during her stay at Sidmouth. A boy was shooting sparrows close to the Duke of Kent's residence, and a shot came through the nursery window, where the Princess was sitting in her nurse's lap, and narrowly escaped hitting her head.

I am indebted to Miss Kortright, an old inhabitant of Kensington, for some pretty little incidents relating to this period of the Queen's life. The Princess was known to go with her mother and her step-sister, Feodore, to a milliner's shop in Kensington, buy a new hat, stay while it was trimmed, and carry it home in her hand quite proudly — but surely it was the old one she carried in her hand! Meeting the Princess in her pony-chaise one day, an "unknown little girl" asked to be allowed to kiss her. The Princess Feodore stopped the tiny carriage and indulged the child's wish. The "unknown little girl" who secured a kiss from her future Queen was Miss Kortright's elder sister.

Mr. Charles Knight, the publisher, has left a pleasing record of this period of the Queen's life. He tells that, during an early morning walk through Kensington Gardens, he saw a group upon the lawn in front of the Palace which seemed to him a "vision of exquisite loveliness." It was the Duchess of Kent and the Princess Victoria breakfasting in the open air, attended by a single page. "What a beautiful characteristic it seemed to me," he writes, "of the training of this royal girl, that she should have been taught not to shrink from the public eye — that she should not have been burdened with a premature conception of her probable high position— that she should enjoy the freedom and simplicity of a child's nature. I passed on and blessed her; and I thank God that I have lived to see the golden fruits of such training."

The education of the Princess Victoria was conducted at first by her mother with the help of Fraulein Lehzen, who at a later date was formally appointed her governess, and remained with the Queen as confidential secretary for a number of years after her accession. The Princess learned her letters at her mother's knee, but not very willingly, and we find Grandmamma of Coburg taking sides with the little truant. She writes to her daughter, "Do not tease your little puss with learning. She is so young still," adding that her grandson, Prince Albert, was making eyes at a picture-book. When it was made clear to the Princess that until the A B C was mastered she could not read books like her mother, she replied with alacrity, "Me learn too, very quick"; and she did, for there was no lack of ability. Her regular education began in her fifth year, when the Rev. George Davys, eventually Bishop of Peterborough, became her tutor. "I fear you will find my little girl very headstrong," explained the Duchess of Kent to the new tutor; "but the ladies of the household will spoil her." As she grew older, the Princess became docile in all things except taking medicine, and she reformed on this point when she discovered that her physician only entertained her with stories after the medicine had been taken. She was reared to speak in French and German as well as in her native tongue. German she found most efficacious when she wanted a favour from her mother. By the time she reached her eleventh year Italian, Latin, Greek, and mathematics had been added to her studies. Music she studied under Mr. John Bernard Sale, afterwards organist at the Chapel Royal, and drawing under Mr. Westall, R.A.

Sketching was a favourite occupation with the Princess, her love of form and of the beauties of nature having been observable at a very early age. When taking walks about Esher with her Uncle Leopold, she often pointed out beautiful bits of landscape, and it was at Claremont that she first began sketching from nature. She was fond too of looking at pictures and of imagining what the people in them might be saying to each other, a dramatic element in her character which found further expression in the mock ceremonies which she enacted with her retinue of dolls. Upon a long board full of pegs, into which the dolls' feet fitted, she rehearsed court receptions, presentations, and held mimic drawing-rooms and levees. Her dolls numbered one hundred and thirty-two; a large number of them were dressed entirely by herself in artistic costumes to represent historic characters or people she knew. A list of them, with their names and history, was kept in a copybook. She was passionately fond of animals and of seeing natural history collections; her first visit to the British Museum was an unbounded joy, and she begged to be taken there often. Botany too delighted her, and she began the study, under the tuition of her Uncle Leopold, among the bowery groves of Claremont. Lord Albemarle remembers seeing her watering her flowers at Kensington Palace, and tells that it was amusing to see how impartially she divided the contents of her watering-pot between the flowers and her own little feet.

And so the childhood of the Queen passed under the watchful eye of that wisest of mothers, and year by year saw her fine natural abilities developing, and her character ripening into thoughtful maidenhood. As yet no busybody had been allowed to disturb the simplicity of her child's nature by whispering in her ear, "You are the future Queen of England." She had been reared in all things to be a queen, without being oppressed or unduly elated by a knowledge of the high position to which she might attain. In closing this period of the Queen's life, we can but echo the words of Grandmamma of Coburg, who, writing to the Duchess of Kent upon the Princess's eleventh birthday, says: "My blessings and good wishes for the day which gave you the sweet blossom of May! May God preserve and protect the valuable life of that lovely flower from all the dangers that will beset her mind and heart! The rays of the sun are scorching at the height to which she may one day attain. It is only by the blessing of God that all the fine qualities He has put into that young soul can be kept pure and untarnished."

THE GIRLHOOD OF QUEEN VICTORIA

THE day on which the Queen was told that she was heiress to the throne of Great Britain may be regarded as marking that period in her life when she emerged from mere childhood into the more thoughtful period of girlhood. This occurred when she was approaching her twelfth birthday. Two years previously, Sir Walter Scott, after dining with the Duchess of Kent, noted in his diary that the "little Victoria is educated with much care, and watched so closely that no busy maid has a moment to whisper, 'You are heir of England.'" There are several accounts of the manner in which the information was first conveyed to the young Princess. It was current gossip of the time that Prince George of Cumberland, who was fond of teasing his pretty cousin, twitted her one day with the unpleasant prospect of having to be a queen, enlarging on the discomforts of the position, and throwing out dark hints of the untimely end of Mary Queen of Scots. If the Princess failed in her lessons, or was discovered in a delinquency, Prince George improved the occasion by saying, "A pretty sort of queen you will make." All such references were received by the Princess with passionate tears.

Another version is given by Caroline Fox. Writing in her journal, she details a gossipy visit from her friend Mrs. Corgie, the "rightful Lady George Murray," who told her that the Princess Victoria was first informed of the high position which awaited her by her mother. The Duchess of Kent desired that her daughter should read aloud that portion of English history which related to the death of the Princess Charlotte. In reading, the Princess made a dead halt, and asked if it were possible that she should ever be Queen. Her mother replied: "As this is a very possible circumstance, I am anxious to bring you up as a good woman, when you will be a good queen also."

It appears also that the Princess's governess, the Baroness Lehzen, and her tutor, the Rev. George Davys, both claim to have informed their pupil of her place in the succession to the throne. In a letter written in her eighty-fourth year by the Baroness to her former pupil, she says: "I ask your Majesty's leave to cite some remarkable words of your Majesty when only twelve years old, while the Regency Bill was in progress. I then said to the Duchess of Kent that now for the first time your Majesty ought to know your place in the succession. Her Royal Highness agreed with me, and I put the genealogical table into the historical book." The Baroness continues her story to the effect that when the Princess opened the book and noticed the additional paper, she said, "I never saw that before."

"'It was not thought necessary you should, Princess,' the governess replied.

"'I see,' continued the Princess, 'I am nearer the throne than I thought.'

"'So it is, madam,' replied the Baroness.

"After some moments, the Princess answered, 'Now, many a child would boast, but they don't know the difficulty. There is much splendour, but there is more responsibility'; and laying her hand in that of her governess, she said, 'I will be good. I understand now why you urged me so much to learn even Latin.'"

The Baroness then explained to the Princess that her aunt, Queen Adelaide, might yet have children, in which case she would not succeed to the throne.

"And if it were so," replied the Princess, "I should never feel disappointed, for I know by the love Aunt Adelaide bears me how fond she is of children."

I am indebted to the Rev. Canon Davys, son of the Queen's tutor, Bishop Davys, for yet another account of how the momentous tidings were conveyed to the Princess Victoria.

"The story of the Princess discovering that she would be Queen," Canon Davys tells me, "has not generally been correctly told. My father had set her to make a chart of the kings and queens. She got as far as 'Uncle William.' Next day my father said to the Princess, 'But you have not put down the next heir to the throne.' She rather hesitated, and said, 'I hardly like to put down myself.' My father mentioned the matter to the Duchess of Kent, who said she was so glad that the truth had come upon her daughter in this way, as it was time she became aware what responsibility was awaiting her."

The three accounts agree in showing that the Princess's mother, together with her governess and her tutor, all felt, after the accession of William IV., that the time had arrived for the Princess to be informed of her position, and that each of them made a lesson in history the means by which to tell her. As to whether Prince George of Cumberland had previously let the proverbial a "cat out of the bag" remains a moot point.

The Princess Victoria was now regarded by the people as the heiress-apparent; but the King himself never ceased hoping that a child of his own might yet be born to succeed, and at times he displayed jealousy of his niece of Kent and ill-will towards the mother who had borne her. In beautiful contrast was the attitude of the Good Queen Adelaide. When her second child died, soon after the birth of the Princess Victoria, she wrote to the Duchess of Kent, "My children are dead, but yours lives, and she is mine too."

A Court lady recalls a pleasing little incident which she witnessed when Queen Adelaide was still Duchess of Clarence. The lady was sitting with Her Royal Highness, when the Duchess of Kent and the Princess Victoria were announced, whereupon she rose to withdraw.

"Do not go yet," said the Duchess of Clarence. "I want you to see little Victoria; she is such a sweet child."

After drawing the Princess towards her with affectionate greeting, the Duchess of Clarence produced a child's tea-service of the prettiest china imaginable, which, in her sweet, kind way, she had provided as a surprise for her little niece. Trivial as the incident is, nothing could better illustrate the love of the childless Queen for the heiress to the throne.

The Princess Victoria attended her first Drawing-Room on the 24th of February, 1831, on the occasion of Queen Adelaide's birthday. It was a reception of unusual splendour; nothing had been seen like it since the Drawing-Room at which the Princess Charlotte had been presented on the occasion of her marriage. There were three things to make it of special import: it was the first Drawing-Room held after the accession of William IV., it was Queen Adelaide's birthday, and the first formal appearance at Court of the Heiress of Great Britain.

The Princess set out from Kensington Palace with her mother, attended by a suite of ladies and gentlemen in State carriages, and escorted by a detachment of Life Guards. This was our beloved Queen's first public procession, and the number in which she has taken part since it would indeed be difficult to enumerate. Some of the people, as they watched her, cheered, and others wept, for there was something both joyous and pathetic in the sight of this young girl upon whose head the weight of a crown might fall all too soon. At the Drawing-Room she was the centre of observation. She stood on Queen Adelaide's left hand, dressed in a frock of English blonde draped over white satin. Her fair hair was arranged Madonna-like, according to the fashion of the times, and the braids were fastened at the back of her head with a diamond clasp. Around her throat she wore a single row of lovely pearls. It was no small ordeal for a young girl of twelve, reared in the strictest seclusion, to pass through; but she bore herself with modest dignity, and took evident delight in watching the presentations. The gay scene was as novel to her as to the simplest girl in the land.

Two months later another opportunity was taken by Queen Adelaide of giving prominence to the Princess. The Queen and the royal ladies were standing on the balcony watching the pageant which attended William IV. on the prorogation of his first Parliament. As the people cheered, Queen Adelaide took the young Princess Victoria by the hand, and, leading her to the front of the balcony, presented her to the assembled crowds. It would be difficult to decide whether the deafening shouts which rent the air were given more in honour of the future Queen or in recognition of the Good Queen Adelaide's attitude towards the young girl. In the same year the Princess made her first appearance at the theatre, attending a children's entertainment at Covent Garden. A staid chronicler of this event would have us believe that the pleasure which the Princess evinced at seeing a play was rather the result of musical sympathy with the orchestra than of attachment to the drama. Why, then, Mr. Chronicler, did she not go to a concert instead?

The Princess Victoria having been brought so far into prominence, there was much comment regarding her absence from the Coronation of King William IV. and Queen Adelaide in Westminster Abbey, September, 1831. Many reasons were assigned for this omission. Some said that the King, jealous of the attention which the Princess had excited during the last few months, would not assign her the place in the procession due to her rank as the heiress-presumptive. On the other hand, it was affirmed that the Duchess of Kent pleaded the delicate state of her young daughter's health as an excuse for keeping her away from the ceremonial. It is a matter of history that there was always friction between the Duchess of Kent and the King regarding the comparative seclusion in which the Princess was kept. The Duchess was determined to preserve the girlish innocence and purity of her daughter by withholding her as much as possible from the Court. The King was well known for a coarse wit. When he was in a good humour "he swore like an admiral," and when he was in a bad humour "he swore like our armies in Flanders." His facetious extravagances at the dinner table were the gossip of the time. Still, his sailor-like bluntness and cheery jocosity made him, in spite of his easy morals, a favourite with the populace, and there were many who blamed the Duchess of Kent for persistently opposing him. We find a morning journal reproving her in plain terms for her "impertinence" in keeping her daughter away from the Coronation.

The confidence and esteem with which the Duchess of Kent was regarded, however, by the nation was amply testified by the action of Parliament in appointing her to be Regent in the event of the Princess Victoria succeeding to the throne before she came of age. The Regency Bill was passed immediately after the accession of William IV., and during its discussion Cabinet ministers vied with each other in praising the admirable training given by the Duchess of Kent to her daughter. An extract from the speech of Lord Lyndhurst will illustrate the general feeling: "The first question which your lordships will naturally ask is, whom do we propose as the guardian of Her Royal Highness under the circumstances inferred? I am sure, however, that the answer will at once suggest itself to every mind. It would be quite impossible that we should recommend any other individual for that high office than the illustrious Princess, the mother of H.R.H. the Princess Victoria. The manner in which Her Royal Highness the Duchess of Kent has hitherto discharged her duty in the education of her illustrious offspring — and I speak upon the subject not from vague report, but from accurate information — gives us the best ground to hope most favourably of H.R. Highness's future conduct. Looking at the past, it is evident that we cannot find a better guardian for the time to come."

After the passing of the Regency Bill, we find another of those charming letters from Grandmamma of Coburg to her daughter. "It is only a just return," she writes to the Duchess of Kent, "for your constant devotion and care to your child. May God bless and protect our little darling. If I could but once see her again! The print you sent me of her is not like the dear picture I have. The quantity of curls hide the well-shaped head, and make it look too large for the lovely little figure."

The tender family circle of the Princess seemed to be narrowing sadly at this period of her early girlhood. Her favourite paternal uncle, the Duke of York, had died; her half-sister, the Princess Feodore, had married the Prince of Hohenlohe and had left England; and in 1831 her beloved Grandmamma of Coburg died. About the same time her Uncle Leopold succeeded to the throne of Belgium. This was perhaps the greatest grief of all, bringing to an end as it did her delightful visits to Claremont. The Queen has herself told us that she "adored" her Uncle Leopold, and his departure from the country filled her with despair. From the hour of her father's death he had been her watchful guardian, advising her mother in all points regarding her training, and even providing additional income. The Princess was a warm-hearted girl, passionate in her attachments, as she has remained throughout her life, and one can understand that the break up of so many family ties oppressed her spirits at this time. She had few of the outlets of ordinary girls for throwing dull care aside, the circumstance of her high estate keeping her life monotonous and lonely. When I asked one who knew the Princess well as a girl what her amusements were, he replied that they were all of a quiet kind — chiefly walking in Kensington Gardens, driving her ponies, and playing with her favourite dog Dash, a black-and-tan spaniel. In order to vary this rather too quiet existence, the Duchess of Kent took her daughter on a series of visits to places of interest in her native land. In these days of varied travel, one marvels to find that Her Majesty never set foot off English soil, if we except Wales, until she had been several years upon the throne, and was both wife and mother.

The royal visitors could not enjoy Brighton by reason of the crowds which dogged their footsteps; but at Broadstairs they spent some pleasant times, residing at Pierpont House; and Ramsgate was always a favourite watering-place. In 1830, the Princess spent a long holiday at Malvern, where she led a free outdoor life, and displayed agility in climbing walls and trees. Unfortunately she did not descend with equal ease, and on one occasion had to be rescued from the bough of an apple tree by the gardener. At Tunbridge Wells the old people recall her fearless donkey-riding, and her fondness for coming to drink the water from the widow who kept the well. There comes a story, too, that her mother would not allow her to outrun her exchequer by the purchase of a half-crown box until she had the money to pay for it, her rather reckless purchase of presents for her friends having reduced the Princess to a temporary state of insolvency. When her next allowance of pocket-money became due, she set forth on her donkey at seven o'clock in the morning to claim the box, which the shopkeeper had retained for her.

She was also taken on visits to country seats; and the story is told that during a visit to Wentworth House the Princess was a little too adventurous in racing about the glades and unfrequented parts of the grounds, heedless of the warning which the gardener had given her that they were "slape." "What is 'slape'?" asked the Princess, receiving when she had scarcely uttered the words a practical demonstration as her feet slided from under her on the slippery path. "That is slape, miss," replied the old gardener, with a sense of humour, as he assisted her to her feet.

A note from the diary of Thomas Moore gives a peep behind the scenes when the royal travellers were expected at Watson Taylor's place, near Devizes. "Have been invited," he writes, "to meet the Duchess of Kent and young Victoria... rather amused with being behind the scenes to see the fuss of preparation for a royal reception." He then proceeds to describe a musical evening, the Duchess and the Princess singing duets together. "No attempts at bravura and graces," is his criticism, "but all simplicity and expression. Her Royal Highness evidently is very fond of music, and would have gone on singing much longer if there had not been rather premature preparations for bed." To have pleased the ear of so fastidious a judge as Thomas Moore proves that the Princess had a sweet and well-trained voice.

Even during these early jaunts the Princess took part in public functions. We find her opening the Victoria Park at Bath, and distributing colours to a regiment of foot at Plymouth, and later on, when she visited Wales, she gave the prizes to the successful competitors at the Eisteddfod.

In 1832, the Princess was taken on a further tour, which, being attended with some ceremonious arrangement, caused the old King to speak with amused cynicism of his niece's jaunts as "royal progresses." The Duchess of Kent and the Princess, attended by a modest retinue, set forth in carriages from Kensington Palace, travelling by way of Shrewsbury and Coventry, into Wales. They crossed the Menai Strait, enjoying the lovely scenery at their leisure, and passing over the water to Anglesey made a prolonged stay in the island, returning home by way of the Midland counties. An opportunity was taken in passing through the manufacturing towns to show the Princess the interiors of some of the factories. It is amusing to find, in records of the period, that the interest which she took in what was shown her is gravely interpreted as evidence of her desire to promote British industries. The fact that she was delighted with a working model illustrating cotton-spinning is commented upon as though our beloved Queen had been a second Arkwright come to judgment, instead of a bright, clever girl full of curiosity. During this tour the Duchess of Kent and her daughter paid visits to several historic country seats, among them Eaton Hall, Chatsworth, Alton Towers, and Powis Castle. Wherever they appeared the people came out in great crowds to see them, testifying their loyalty to the young Heiress of Britain. The King indeed was not far wrong when he testily spoke of these visits as "royal progresses," for, however desirous the Duchess of Kent might have been to make the Princess's journeys private, the people insisted upon openly displaying their loyalty.

In 1833, the Duchess and her daughter resided for some months at Norris Castle in the Isle of Wight, where the Princess was frequently seen enjoying country rambles, or listening to the stories of the sailors and the coastguardsmen as she lingered about the shore. A pretty incident is told by an American writer who was visiting the island. While in Arreton churchyard, near Brading, he noticed a lady and a little girl seated near the grave of the "Dairyman's Daughter." The lady was reading aloud the story of the humble heroine, and as the visitor regarded the pair he could see that the large blue eyes of the young girl were suffused with tears. He subsequently learned that the ladies were the Duchess of Kent and the Princess Victoria. It was doubtless during this visit of her girlhood that the

Queen formed an affection for the Isle of Wight, which induced her, in later years, to select Osborne as a marine residence.

After a period of rest at Norris Castle, the Duchess of Kent and her daughter went on board their yacht, the Emerald, for a cruise in the Channel, visiting Southampton, Plymouth, and Torquay. At each place they were welcomed by loyal addresses from the local authorities. The enthusiasm of the people was great; and if the old King had been annoyed at the homage paid to the mother and daughter during their tour by land, he was more chagrined than ever by the popular demonstrations of loyalty which attended their progress by water. He sent forth a royal decree that an end should be put to the continual "poppings" of the ships in the Channel in the way of salutes to the Duchess of Kent's yacht. The naval authorities were of opinion that the royal ladies were legally entitled to the salutes, whereupon the irate King endeavoured to coerce the Duchess into waiving her right to them; but Her Royal Highness replied with becoming dignity: "If the King would offer me a slight in the face of his people, he can offer it so easily that he should not ask me to make the task easier." We fear there were young midshipmen irreverent enough to cry, "That's 'one' for the King," as they tossed their caps in the air and gave three cheers for the pretty, blue-eyed Princess, who was so merrily sailing the waters of the Channel under the care of her dignified mamma. The King finally ended the miserable contention by summoning the Privy Council to pass an order that henceforth no salute should be offered to any vessel flying the royal flag unless the King or the Queen were on board. The Court chronicler very fittingly describes this as a "council for a foolish business."

It was during her cruise on the Emerald that the Princess met with her third narrow escape from death. She was sitting on deck when the yacht came into collision with another vessel so violently that the top-mast of the Emerald fell close to the Princess, and would have struck her but for the timely intervention of the pilot, Mr. Saunders, who snatched her up in his arms and carried her to a place of safety. The Queen never forgot her gallant preserver. She promoted him to the rank of Master when she ascended the throne, and cared for his widow and children after his death.

While the Princess was thus expanding her mind by travel, her general education was being pursued with strictest care. After the passing of the Regency Bill, and the public recognition of the Princess as heiress-presumptive, Parliament granted an extra £10,000 a year for her education. Her resident governess from childhood was Fraulein Lehzen, the daughter of a Hanoverian clergyman, who came first to Kensington Palace as the instructress of the Princess Feodore. She was made a Baroness by George IV. in recognition of her services to the Princess Victoria. The Queen has related that she regarded her with the warmest affection, although she stood much in awe of her. It has already been told how the Baroness acquainted her pupil with her nearness to the throne, and it would appear from the Baroness's letters of this period that she had been absent for a time from Kensington Palace, and returned there from Paris in May, 1831. "My Princess," she writes, "will be twelve years old to-morrow. She is not tall, but very pretty, has dark blue eyes, and a mouth which, though not tiny, is very good-tempered and pleasant, very fine teeth, a small but graceful figure, and a very small foot. She was dressed (to receive me) in white muslin with a coral necklet. Her whole bearing is so childish and engaging that one could not desire a more amiable child." Again she writes, shortly afterwards, that her Princess "flourishes in goodness and beauty."

It was now thought, however, desirable by the King that an English governess should be appointed for the Princess in conjunction with the Baroness, and His Majesty selected for this important post Charlotte Florentia (Clive), third Duchess of Northumberland and second daughter of the first Earl of Powis. It was the duty of the Duchess to instruct her pupil in matters of Court etiquette and ceremonial, to train her in deportment, and to generally instruct her in the lighter graces. How apt was the pupil and how well the instructress succeeded in her delicate task was evinced by the almost startling ease and grace of manner which distinguished the girl-Queen when she first ascended the throne. It is the universal testimony of all who have been about the Queen that she is unsurpassed for graciousness and queenly bearing. Madame Bourdin instructed her in dancing, and the famous vocalist, Luigi Lablache, in singing. The Princess must surely have derived some entertainment from her singing-master, for he is reported to have been of such huge dimensions that one of his boots would have made a small portmanteau, and a child might have been clad in one of his gloves. His portentous voice rang through the house like a great bell. His wife is said to have been aroused by a sound in the middle of the night which she took for the tocsin announcing a fire; but it was only Lablache producing in his sleep these bell-like sounds.

Mr. Bernard Sale continued to instruct the Princess in music, and Mr. Richard Westall, R.A., in drawing and painting, in which she grew so proficient that, had she been "Miss" instead of the Princess Victoria, her tutor was of opinion that she would have been the first woman artist of the day. She once told her tutor that her pencil was a source of great delight to her, and that it was a study in which she would willingly spend more of her time than in any other. This talent has been inherited by all the Queen's daughters, but more especially by the Princess Louise, who is both artist and sculptor. Mr. Stewart, the writing and arithmetic-master at

Westminster School, instructed the Princess in those branches of education.

From the well-known riding-master of the day, Mr. Fozard, the Princess was rapidly acquiring that grace in the saddle of which old people never tire of speaking, as they recall the days when they saw the girl-Queen cantering down the Row. Her mother was her chief instructress in languages; Mr. Amos trained her in the difficult paths of constitutional history; while her chief preceptor in Greek, Latin, mathematics, theology, and literature continued to be her childhood's tutor, the Rev. George Davys, who had been made Dean of Chester, and was eventually to be Bishop of Peterborough. The Queen constantly speaks of him as "my kind, good master." The Duchess of Kent thought very highly of her daughter's tutor, who also served as domestic chaplain at Kensington Palace. An amusing story used to be told by him. "I like your sermons so much, Mr. Dean," said the Duchess one day, adding, as he bowed low, "because they are so short." I am indebted to his son, Canon Davys, for a corrected version of the story. What the Duchess really said was that she liked the Dean's sermons because they were so good and so short. Bishop Davys' modesty or his sense of humour led him to omit the word "good" when he told the story.

The reverend tutor had a quiet humour, and enjoyed his pupil's clever repartees. The Dean had been preaching from his favourite text, "Whatsoever a man soweth, that shall he also reap." The Princess asked, "Do not men reap anything but what they sow?" "Yes," replied the Dean, "if they allow some one to come and sow tares amongst their wheat." "Ah, I know who that some one is," said the Princess, "and I must keep him at arm's length." "At arm's length only, your Royal Highness?" rejoined the Dean. "Well, if I keep him there, he won't do much harm," was the quick reply.

Bishop Davys was fond of telling another story as illustrating his young pupil's fearless truthfulness. The Princess had been giving trouble to her tutor over her lessons one morning, and the Baroness Lehzen had occasion to reprove her. When the Duchess of Kent came into the room, she inquired after her daughter's behaviour. The Baroness reported that the Princess had been naughty once. But the little culprit interrupted her with, "Twice, Lehzen; don't you remember?" A less partial judge than Bishop Davys might have discovered a little sauciness in this very truthful statement.

The Bishop was an exceedingly good elocutionist, and it is to his careful training that the Princess owed her clear and expressive intonation. She was very fond of good literature, and read principally in the English classics; Pope, Dryden, and Shakespeare being special favourites. The

"Spectator" was the class book chiefly used by the Princess, and she also read the Latin authors under her tutor's direction. To him also she looked for religious guidance in the solemn ceremony of confirmation, for which she was now preparing. There is every evidence to show that her feelings at this period were of a serious and devout kind. On the 30th of August, 1835, the Princess stood in her simple white confirmation dress in the Chapel Royal of St. James's. The Archbishop of Canterbury and the Bishop of London officiated at the ceremony, which was entirely private. There were present the King and Queen, the Duchess of Kent, the Duchess of Saxe-Weimar, and several other members of the royal family. The address of the Archbishop was tender and solemn, and as he dwelt upon the obligations of her high estate, and impressively commended her to the guidance of the Almighty Ruler of the universe, the Princess turned to her mother, and laying her head upon her bosom, sobbed with emotion; a sight which brought tears to the eyes of most who were present.

During the past year the Princess had been in a delicate state of health; in fact, at the close of her fifteenth year her condition caused general concern. When, after her recovery, she was again seen driving with her mother in Hyde Park, the demonstration of joy shown by the people amounted to an ovation. We find her now emerging from the unformed period of girlhood into maidenly maturity and comeliness. She was seen more frequently at public places of amusement, and her fresh, fair face, peeping from under the huge bonnet of the period, was the delight of the London crowds. The extreme simplicity of attire which had distinguished her as a child was exchanged for rich and tasteful costumes. In the summer of 1835, she accompanied Queen Adelaide to the Ascot races, and as she drove in the royal procession to the racecourse her pretty appearance was much talked of. She wore a large pink bonnet and a rose-coloured satin frock, which matched the roses on her cheeks and contrasted nicely with her fair hair and blue eyes. Mr. Nathaniel Parker Willis, the American writer, then visiting London, has recorded his impressions of the Princess as he saw her at Ascot. He came to the conclusion that she was quite "unnecessarily pretty and interesting" for a royal princess. "She will be sold, poor thing!" continues this youth of eighteen, "bartered away by those great dealers in royal hearts, whose calculations will not be of much consolation to her if she happens to have a taste of her own." Not so fast, Mr. Willis; the Prince Charming will shortly appear to woo and win the fair Princess in the pink bonnet and the rose-coloured dress, and she has "a taste of her own, and will show it."

In the autumn of this year the Princess and her mother made another "royal progress," this time through East Anglia. Loyal demonstrations met them everywhere, and at King's Lynn the railway navvies took the horses from the carriage and drew it for some distance. At Burghley great preparations were made for their reception. Mr. Greville records that all passed off well at the official dinner, except that a pail of ice was "landed" by a nervous waiter in the Duchess of Kent's lap, which made a great bustle. The Court chronicler does not say so, but we are afraid the Princess laughed at the contretemps. A ball followed, which was opened by Lord Exeter and the Princess, who after dancing one dance went to bed; the Duchess never allowing any festivity to interfere with the simple routine of her daughter's life. Next day the royal ladies set off to Holkham, where they were the guests of the Lady Anne Coke. Separate bedrooms had been prepared for the Princess and her mother; but the Duchess desired that a bed should be provided for her daughter in her own room, as they never slept apart. The Earl of Albemarle, who came to assist his sister, Lady Anne Coke, to entertain the royal visitors, records in his autobiography that the Princess "had most sweet and winning manners."

In May, 1836, when the Princess was seventeen, there came to Kensington Palace some very interesting visitors — the Duke of Coburg and his two sons, Ernest and Albert. It was the first meeting of the Princess Victoria and her cousin Prince Albert. Fond relatives had destined the two for each other from their cradles; but the happiness of the Princess was too dear both to her mother and to her uncle, King Leopold, for any coercion to be used. It was arranged for the young people to meet without reference being made to any tenderer tie than that of cousinship. They passed several weeks in each other's society, playing duets on the piano, sketching, walking and riding in Kensington Gardens, and attending some functions in town. Prince Albert, writing home regarding this visit, said: "Dear aunt is very kind to us, and does everything she can to please us, and our cousin also is very amiable." The Queen, in after years, gave the following description of her husband at this period: "The Prince was at this time very handsome, but very stout, which he entirely grew out of afterwards. He was most amiable, natural, unaffected, and merry — full of interest in everything." Baron Stockmar, that judicious person whose business it was to attentively scrutinise the Prince Albert, had already reported to "Uncle Leopold" that he was endowed with the personal characteristics "likely to please the sex," and that his mental qualities were also of a high order.

At the end of a month the Duke of Coburg and his sons left Kensington and returned to Germany. The Princess parted from each of her cousins with equal affectionateness, but we find that Prince Albert is mentioned with special tenderness in a letter to her Uncle Leopold. Prince Albert too, during his Continental travels, which followed the visit to Kensington, collected views of the places which he visited, and sent them in an album to the Princess, together with a rose gathered from the top of the Rigi. Now a rose is a rose the whole world over when passed between man and maid, even though it be a dried one from the top of the Rigi. Still we are told that there was nothing between Princess Victoria and her handsome cousin at this time. It was well known that the King did not favour such an alliance for his niece, and was disposed to give his help to one of the other suitors, for, like "Portia," the young Princess was bewildered by the number of Princes who came wooing. There were five suitors at this time besides Prince Albert. We find a letter of the period in which an application is made on behalf of Prince Adalbert of Prussia that he might be permitted "to place himself on the list of those who pretend to the hand of the Princess Victoria." The Duchess of Kent replied that such an application must be referred to the King, adding, "But if I know my duty to the King, I know also my maternal ones, and I am of opinion that the Princess should not marry till she is much older." So in the meantime Prince Albert was travelling and studying in order to be a fit consort, if fortune favoured him, for the Queen of Great Britain; the other five suitors were kept at a distance, and the Princess continued to live her happy, quiet life at Kensington Palace.

On the 21st of August, 1836, the King celebrated his seventy-first birthday by a State dinner, at which the Princess Victoria occupied a prominent position. Unfortunately it proved to be the most terrible ordeal through which the Princess had yet passed. The King in his after-dinner speech made this cruel thrust at the Duchess of Kent. "I trust in God," he said, "that my life may be spared nine months longer, after which period, in event of my death, no regency will take place. I shall then have the satisfaction of leaving the royal authority to the personal exercise of that young lady" (here the King indicated the Princess Victoria, who sat on the opposite side of the table), "the heiress-presumptive of the Crown, not in the hands of a person now near to me" (here the King turned in an angry manner and glanced at the Duchess of Kent, who sat at his side). He continued his angry tirade, to the effect that he had been insulted by the Duchess having kept away her daughter from his Court, and commanded that in future the Princess should upon all occasions appear. The Duchess of Kent received this brutal outburst with dignified silence, but the warm-hearted Princess burst into tears. After dinner the Duchess ordered her carriage, and was about to depart with her daughter; but by the intercession of the Good Queen Adelaide she was prevailed upon to remain at the Castle for the night.

Nine months later, on the 24th of May, 1837, the Princess Victoria attained her legal majority. This, her eighteenth birthday, was celebrated with every demonstration of regard and attachment by the inhabitants of Kensington. At six o'clock the Union Jack was hoisted at the summit of the old church on the green opposite the Palace; while from the Palace itself floated a flag of pure white silk, upon which was embroidered in letters of blue, "Victoria." Never had the old Court suburb looked gayer. Flags and colours were displayed from every house along the High Street, and as early as six o'clock in the morning the crowds began to throng into Kensington Gardens. At seven o'clock a serenade was performed beneath the windows of the Princess's room; and all through the day the great world of London flocked to Kensington Palace to pay congratulatory homage to the heiress-apparent, who would ere long be Queen, for the King was fast nearing his end; he was, indeed, so ill that their Majesties could not take part in the festivities. At night a State ball of unequalled splendour was given at St. James's Palace, and opened by the Princess with a quadrille, in which she danced with Lord Fitzalan, eldest son of the Earl of Surrey, and grandson of the Duke of Norfolk. It was observed by the guests that the Princess now took precedence of her mother, occupying the chair of State between the dances. During the days which followed came congratulatory addresses from the municipal authorities throughout the country, and one from the City of London. The King presented his niece with a handsome grand piano, and many beautiful and costly presents were sent to her from all parts of the empire. Ten days later a Drawing-Room was held to celebrate the Princess's majority, and this proved to be her last appearance at Court as the Princess Victoria. With her womanhood came also her queenhood.

THE MAIDEN MONARCH

ON the 17th of June, 1837, it was rumoured in Court circles that His Majesty King William IV. was rapidly sinking, and that the Archbishop had gone to Windsor to administer the last Sacrament. Three days later came the tidings, "The King is dead." He expired shortly after two o'clock in the morning; and without loss of time my Lord Archbishop Howley and the Chamberlain, Lord Conyngham, left Windsor, and took coach for London to announce to the Princess Victoria her accession to the throne of the British Empire. The old king of seventy-six was succeeded by the maiden of eighteen.

Driving post haste along the silent roads, in the opening dawn of the June morning, the Lord Primate and the Lord Chamberlain reached Kensington Palace at five o'clock. All was silent, save the singing of the birds, who fittingly were the first of living creatures to serenade the Maiden Monarch, as eighteen years ago they had welcomed her birth, in the same old Palace, with similar song. The lordly messengers had much ado to awake the sleeping household. They knocked, they rang, they thumped for a considerable time before they could rouse the porter at the gates, and they were again kept waiting in the courtyard. Finally, after much ringing of bells, the attendant of the Princess Victoria appeared, and informed their lordships that her royal mistress was in such a sweet sleep that she could not venture to disturb her. Then said they: "We are come to the Queen on business of State, and even her sleep must give way to that." It did; and, to prove that she did not keep them waiting, "in a few minutes she came into the room in a loose white nightgown and shawl, her nightcap thrown off, and her hair falling upon her shoulders, her feet in slippers, tears in her eyes, but perfectly collected and dignified."

This piquant bit of description, regarding the young Queen's appearance, is from Miss Wynn's "Diaries of a Lady of Quality"; and although it is repeated by most biographers of Her Majesty, and has been given the dignity of historic record by Mr. Justin McCarthy in his "History of Our Own Times," it must not be overlooked that Mr. Greville, Clerk of the Council, who arrived at the Palace a few hours later, and received his information from the Lord Chamberlain, relates that, "On the morning of the King's death the Archbishop of Canterbury and Lord Conyngham arrived at Kensington at five o'clock, and immediately desired to see 'the Queen.' They were ushered into an apartment, and in a few minutes the door opened, and she came in wrapped in a dressing-gown, and with slippers on her naked feet." We are inclined to think that the Queen would and did put on her dressing-gown before giving audience to the Primate and Chamberlain, although in the excitement of the occasion some one may have mistaken it for her nightdress. In 1863, when Dean Stanley was on a visit to Osborne, he asked Her Majesty if she would give him an account of how the news of her accession was conveyed to her, which she did in the following words: "It was about 6 a.m. that mamma came and called me, and said I must go to see Lord Conyngham directly — alone. I got up, put on my dressing-gown, and went into a room where I found Lord Conyngham, who knelt and kissed my hand, and gave me the certificate of the King's death. In an hour from that time Baron Stockmar came. He had been sent over by King Leopold on hearing of the King's dangerous illness. At 2 p.m. that same day I went to the Council led by my two uncles, the King of Hanover and the Duke of Cambridge." All accounts agree that, immediately the momentous tidings of her accession were conveyed to the Queen, she turned to the Primate, and said, "I ask your Grace to pray for me." And so was begun, with the tears and prayers of a pure young girl, the glorious reign of Victoria.

Immediately after the announcement had been made to the Queen of her accession preparations were made at Kensington Palace for the holding of her first Council. Many who were present at that most memorable Board have recorded their testimony to the admirable composure of the young girl suddenly called to such a trying ordeal. "Had she been my own daughter," said the Duke of Wellington, "I could not have wished to see her play her part better"; and Sir Robert Peel, speaking of the Queen's demeanour, said: "There is something which art cannot make and which lessons cannot teach; there was that in her demeanour which could only be suggested by a high and generous nature." A little incident occurred during the administration of the Oath for the security of the Church of Scotland which showed that the young Queen was not disposed to be overawed by her Ministers. When she had occasion to recapitulate the title of an old Act of Parliament in which the word "intitulated" was used instead of "entitled," Lord Melbourne, standing by her side, said, "Entitled, please, your Majesty." She turned quickly towards him with a look of surprise, and looking again at the paper repeated in a louder voice, "An Act intitulated." When the Council was over, she went to her mother's room, and with deep emotion expressed her inability to realise that she really was Queen, and requested that she should be left absolutely alone for two hours to think over the responsibilities lying before her.

To the Good Queen Adelaide, who had been to her like a second mother, the young Queen showed the most thoughtful regard. Almost her first act, after meeting the Council, was to write to the sorrowing widow a letter of affectionate condolence, which she addressed to "Her Majesty the Queen," delicately refusing to remind her aunt that she was no longer entitled to that distinction. When Colonel Wood, who was conducting executive business for the Dowager Queen Adelaide, after the funeral of the King, represented to Her Majesty that there were some little things at Windsor Castle which the Dowager would like to retain, she replied, "Oh, Colonel, let the dear Queen have them by all means, and anything else in the Castle which she may desire." Later on, when the young Queen had removed with her Court to Windsor, she noticed that a bed of violets which her Aunt Adelaide had cherished were in bloom, and gave directions for the flowers to be gathered and despatched, with her love, to the widowed Queen. A very simple act, but one which showed that queenhood had not spoiled the simple, loving nature of Victoria.

At ten o'clock, on the morning after her accession, the Queen, accompanied by her mother, and attended by a train of coaches carrying her lords and ladies, and escorted by cavalry, drove to St. James's Palace to be publicly proclaimed. All the avenues leading to the Palace were lined with people, and prominent in one of the balconies was the striking figure of Daniel O'Connell, whose loyalty knew no bounds. While the Proclamation was being read, the "little Queen" stood at the window of the Presence Chamber, in view of the people, a somewhat pathetic figure. She was dressed in deep mourning with white cuffs, a white tippet, and a border of white crape, under what the "Court Chronicle" calls a "small" black bonnet — small for the period of enormous headgear, we may add — which was placed far back on her head, showing her light hair, simply parted over her forehead in the "pure virginal style." She was looking very pale, but retained her composure while the routine of the ceremonial was proceeding. When, however, the cannon began to thunder, the trumpets sounded, the band struck up the National Anthem, and the plaudits of the people, crying, "God Save the Queen," rent the air —

"She saw no purple shine,
For tears had dimmed her eyes;
She only knew her childhood's flowers

Were happier pageantries!
And while the heralds played their parts
Those million shouts to drown —
'God save the Queen,' from hill to mart
She heard through all her beating heart,
And turned and wept;
She wept to wear a crown."

It was but a passing and natural wave of emotion, for we find the "weeping queen" an hour later, with her tears dried, presiding over her Privy Council, with as much ease as though she had been doing nothing else all her life. She afterwards returned to Kensington Palace, and remained in strict seclusion until after the funeral of the late King. A story is told which illustrates the Queen's desire to show fitting respect to the memory of William IV. Sir David Wilkie was commissioned to paint her first Council, and in order to heighten the artistic effect the Queen is represented as wearing a flowing white silk robe, while as a matter of fact she was dressed in a simple mourning dress. It is said that the Queen expressed anxiety over this change in her attire, hoping that it might not be misconstrued as an act of disrespect to the late King, for, she added, "I was in black, notwithstanding." When Wilkie was painting the picture, he had occasion to remark upon the Queen's orderliness. "She appoints a sitting once in two days," he writes, "and she never puts me off." The painter's courtly enthusiasm also leads him to descant upon the lovely form in which the regal power had now appeared. He writes: "Her Majesty is an elegant person; seems to lose nothing of her authority, either by her. youth or delicacy; is approached with the same awe, and obeyed with the same promptitude, as the most commanding of her predecessors."

On the 13th of July the Queen, accompanied by her mother, quitted Kensington, and took up her abode at Buckingham Palace. It must have been a period of sad good-byes, for the young Queen was quitting the home of her birth and the haunts of her childhood, as well as leaving many loyal hearts around whom her own had entwined. No one was forgotten in her leave-takings; even a poor sick girl, the daughter of Hillman, an old servant of her father's, was made happy by the present of a book of Psalms marked with the dates of the days on which the Queen had been accustomed to read them, and in the book was a marker with a peacock worked on it by her own hands.

It was a great contrast from historic Kensington, with its homely surroundings, to the new grandeur of Buckingham Palace; and we fancy the Queen must have experienced a chill of repugnance as she took up her abode there. It is invariably spoken of in the journals of the period as the

"New Palace at Pimlico," for it was not yet quite completed, and workmen were busy night and day fixing the superb bronze entrance gates, preparatory to Her Majesty's arrival. All round was a grey waste of sand which led into dirty roads and squalid alleys. No sooner, however, did the sweet young Queen take up her abode at the New Palace — which everybody said ought to be called the Queen's Palace — than Pimlico, the most desolate suburb in Middlesex, started out of its caterpillar condition, and took wings like a butterfly. Penny barbers burst forth into fashionable perfumers, and tobacconists repainted their wooden Highlanders. The hovels disappeared, and business began to look up. All day long ambassadors' carriages and the equipages of the nobility were careering over the once sandy waste, and it became he most fashionable promenade for all classes. Beauty walked serene in huge round bonnets and voluminous skirts. The beaux were there to admire, dressed in satin waistcoats, tailed coats, with high collars, enormous neckcloths, curled and scented hair, and whiskers of the style known as "mutton chop." A man who had appeared in a moustache would have been scouted by his friends. The nursery-maids no longer stayed under the trees in the adjacent park, but brought their small charges to the confines of the Palace; and soon elderly gentlemen were using strong language — also fashionable — as they tumbled over poodles and small boys, or got their legs entangled in hoops. From eight in the morning until eight at night a crowd waited outside the gates on the chance of seeing the Queen drive out for an airing; and if only a royal servant walked across the courtyard, everybody was in a state of excited expectation.

To those of us who know Her Gracious Majesty only as an elderly woman bowing to her loyal people with a smile a little sad and weary, it is difficult to think of her as the merry young Queen of the thirties, moving about in continuous pageant. The sight of her, in the large round bonnet of the time, with a wreath of daisies or roses inside, framing her fair, girlish face, was indeed sunshine to the crowds who waited daily at Hyde Park Corner to see her drive into the park. Most eyes grew moist at sight of her; she looked so like a child beside her big, elderly aunts and uncles. Mothers loved her because she was such a good daughter; girls adored her because she was one of themselves, and they smoothed and braided their hair to look like the Queen, adopted her favourite colours of pink and blue, and thanked their good fortune if they chanced to be fair, blue-eyed, and petite, while the tall, dark girls were correspondingly unhappy. Wise matrons, mindful of the sad death of the Princess Charlotte with her first-born son, hoped the Queen would not rush into the perils of marriage and maternity too soon, and some even thought it might be safer for her to copy the example of Elizabeth in abjuring wedlock altogether. The young folks did not mind so long as she married for love. The condition of susceptible young men was indeed tragic. Some shot themselves, and some went mad all for love of the virgin Queen. One gentleman of position was reduced to weeding the Round Pond in Kensington Gardens in the hope of obtaining a sight of her, and when the Queen left for Buckingham Palace he had his phaeton in readiness, and drove in front of her carriage all the way to town. He continued to make himself so obtrusive that the authorities were obliged to take him in hand.

Charles Dickens was one of the youths who had a severe attack of Queen fever; happily he recovered, or we should not have received anything from his pen beyond the "Pickwick Papers." His youthful aberration must have come to the great novelist's memory with amusement when, at the climax of his fame, he was commanded to lunch with the Queen at Windsor, and received from her hands a copy of Her Majesty's "Tour in the Highlands," inscribed with the words: "From the humblest to the most distinguished author in England."

Meantime in the New Palace Her Majesty was holding countless functions. A gorgeous new throne, upholstered in crimson velvet with gold trimmings, had been set up, and the gay young Queen tried it, in sportive mood, and said that it was "the most comfortable throne she had ever sat upon." Deputations from the universities, the corporations, and different societies throughout the kingdom trooped to Buckingham Palace to offer her their loyal addresses. Amongst others came a deputation from the Society of Friends, headed by Joseph Sturge, the eminent philanthropist of Birmingham. Never surely were conscientious Quakers placed in more awkward circumstances by reason of their hats. It was clear that they could not enter the royal presence with their hats on, yet — they uncovered not in presence of peasant or of king. What was to be done? There was no red tape about her youthful majesty, and a compromise was made with the sturdy Quakers that as the deputation ascended the grand staircase of Buckingham Palace the Yeomen of the Guard should lift each man's hat for him. Miss Grace Greenwood relates that when she asked Joseph Sturge whether his principles permitted him to kiss the Queen's hand, he answered, "Oh yes, and found that act of homage no hardship, I assure thee. It was a fair, soft, delicate little hand." Another unique ceremony performed by the Queen was presiding over a Chapter of the Order of the Garter for the purpose of bestowing the vacant ribbon on her half-brother, the Prince of Leiningen. The occasion was too tempting for the gossip-mongers, and a story went the round of the papers that the Queen, when arranging her dress for the ceremonial, sent for the venerable Field Marshal, the Duke of Norfolk, and asked with charming naivety "But, my Lord Duke, where am I to wear the garter?" His Grace was able to assure

Her Majesty that it might be worn as an armlet, according to the custom adopted by Queen Anne.

On the 17th of July, scarcely a month after her accession, the Queen prorogued Parliament in person. It was said that the Duchess of Kent and Her Majesty's physician endeavoured to persuade her not to undertake such an exciting ordeal. In fact, the "old folks" about the young Queen undoubtedly showed a disposition to keep her away from great public ceremonials, thinking it not "quite nice" for a young maiden to be exhibited to a thronging populace. They had counted without their host. Victoria had made up her mind to be a queen in fact, and not a mere figure-head, and she quickly proved that she could perform the duties of her high estate without losing anything of her delicacy and modesty as a woman. As for the excitement affecting her health, she laughed merrily at the idea, and bade her physician remember that after her very quiet life she found pageants and ceremonials most diverting. So a splendid new throne was set up in the House of Lords, and around it was blazoned in gold letters "Victoria Regina." The Queen was dressed for the ceremony in a white satin kirtle embroidered in gold, over which was a crimson robe of velvet, trimmed with ermine. The robe was confined at the waist and shoulders with a gold cord and tassels. Her stomacher was a mass of flashing jewels, and she wore diamond bracelets and the armlet of the Garter. On her arrival at the House the upper part of her dress was exchanged for the parliamentary robes of crimson and ermine. She laughed and chatted gaily with her ladies as they robed her, and, preceded by the heralds and lords-in-waiting and attended by all the great officers of State, entered the House, wearing for the first time a diadem upon her brow. She ascended the throne with a firm step, and remained standing and smiling as the lords-in-waiting completed her attire with the mantle of purple velvet. Then in musical accents came the words, "My Lords, be seated," and the time-honoured ceremonial began. The reading of the Queen's speech was the event of the day. "I never heard anything better read in my life than her speech," wrote Charles Sumner, who was present; and the Duke of Sussex, when she had finished, wiped his eyes as he exclaimed, "Beautiful! beautiful!"

As soon as the Queen was settled at Windsor Castle she received a visit from her Uncle Leopold, King of the Belgians, and his consort Louise, daughter of Louis Philippe. One can imagine that the royal hostess spared no pains to fittingly entertain the uncle to whose kindness she owed so much in childhood. The Queen was her own housekeeper, so far as circumstances permitted, and she managed things right royally, but never contracted a debt. She arranged dinner-parties, had delightful impromptu dances, picnics on Virginia Water, organised riding and driving-parties, and got up little evening concerts, at the Castle, at which she frequently sang herself. She was in the saddle most days for two or three hours, attended by a gay cavalcade of ladies and gentlemen. The Queen's passion for riding infected all the women of the country, and is said to have extended even to Lesser Russia. At the Kherson races the ladies rode in caps a la Reine Victoire. Usually the Queen wore a green cloth riding-habit and a black beaver hat; but when, in the autumn, she reviewed the troops in the Home Park, she made quite a martial figure mounted on a splendid grey charger and dressed in a blue cloth coat and skirt and a military cap with a deep gold border. From Windsor she proceeded to Brighton, took possession of the Pavilion, and had a gay time as she took the sea air. She was back again in London in November, and on Lord Mayor's Day made a State entrance into the City, knighted the Mayor and the two Sheriffs (one of whom was Sir Moses Montefiore), and dined at the Guildhall. Never had Gog and Magog looked down upon a fairer guest than the young Queen in her pink and silver brocaded silk gown. A little contretemps happened at the dinner. Her Majesty's lace ruffles, having accidentally become entangled with her bouquet and fan, which, with her smelling-bottle, she had laid on the table beside her plate, were the occasion of breaking the wine-glass from which she had just drunk the toast of the Lord Mayor and the City of London — an accident which caused her some little annoyance. On the 20th of November the Queen opened her first Parliament, and was greeted during her progress to the House by the most loyal demonstrations. The question of the Civil List was settled during the session, and the sum of £385,000 was voted as the annual income for the young sovereign. One of the first things which Her Majesty did with her income was to pay her father's debts, contracted before she was born. It was also said that the Duchess of Kent met with a pleasant surprise one morning when she found on her breakfast table receipts for all outstanding debts. It must be remembered that the Duke of Kent owed his monetary difficulties to his generosity, and that his income was inadequate for a royal duke.

But to turn to the more arduous side of the Queen's life. Upon her accession she made her choice in favour of being a working Queen rather than a show monarch, and it became the duty of her Prime Minister, Lord Melbourne, to instruct her in statecraft. She proved a very apt pupil, and a somewhat trying one too, for she would know the why and wherefore of every document laid before her, and signed nothing until she had read it. When the Prime Minister apologised for bringing so many business despatches, the Queen replied: "My Lord, the attention required from me is only a change of occupation. I have not hitherto led a life of leisure, for I have not long left my lessons." There are many well-known stories about the business exactitude of the young sovereign and of her conscientious scruples; and it is said that Lord Melbourne declared that he "would rather manage ten kings than one queen," notwithstanding that the courtly Melbourne liked his position of chief adviser to a lovely young Queen vastly. He was close upon sixty years of age, cultured, polished, every inch a courtier, a man of the world, and a man of honour. There is no doubt that he was an old beau and devoted to the sex. He had no family of his own, no one to love, and he devoted himself to the young Queen with the affection of a father. He was the leader of the Whig Party, then in power; but even the Tory leaders acknowledged his aptitude for the delicate post of adviser to the Maiden Monarch. The Duke of Wellington said, "I have no small talk, and Peel has no manners, and so the Queen must be left to Melbourne." The Prime Minister's attitude to Her Majesty was far from obsequious, but it conveyed respectful deference, and was winning and sincere. He lived at the Castle, and for the Queen's sake accustomed himself to a mode of life which in other circumstances would have been an intolerable "bore." In the Queen's presence he usually took care only to speak the Queen's English, and pruned his speech of all needless expletives; but on one occasion he forgot himself. He was sitting in his accustomed place at the Queen's left hand at dinner, when the conversation turned upon the recent conversion of Sir Robert Peel and the Tories to Free Trade and the Corn Laws. "Ma'am," said Melbourne excitedly, "it is a —— dishonest act." The ladies-in-waiting were in a state of consternation; but the Queen, with the admirable tact and good sense which always distinguished her, laughingly told her minister that he might discuss the Corn Laws with her in private.

The persons who exercised the chief influence upon the Queen at this time were Baron Stockmar, the trusted friend of her uncle, King Leopold, who had been despatched by him to the British Court to watch over his niece's welfare; the Baroness Lehzen, her former governess, and now her private secretary; the beautiful Duchess of Sutherland, her favourite lady-in-waiting; and, of course, her mother, the Duchess of Kent, who was always her daughter's loved companion, though she took no part in affairs of State. Still, it was to Lord Melbourne that the young Queen always turned for advice. The oracular Stockmar, who became such an important figure in Court circles after Her Majesty's marriage, remained at present in the background. His chief function was to watch "how the wind blew" with regard to Prince Albert of Coburg, the devoted lover whom the coy young Queen was keeping at a distance. In homely phrase, she meant "to enjoy herself for a few years before she got married."

The Queen's life at Windsor was regulated with due regard for her many duties. She rose at eight, breakfasted with her mother — who was so strict in her observance of etiquette that she never came to her Queen-daughter's presence until she was summoned — then, dressed in her white silk robe de chambre, the Queen received Lord Melbourne in her boudoir, read the despatches, and transacted State business. Later in the morning she gave audience, when necessary, to Cabinet Ministers. At two o'clock she rode out, generally at full gallop, attended by her numerous suite, and with Lord Melbourne on her left hand. After riding she amused herself with music and singing and playing with the children, if there were any staying in the Castle. At eight o'clock she entered the room where the guests were assembled for dinner, spoke to each lady, bowed to the men, and, taking the arm of the most distinguished man present, walked into the dining-room. The Queen had one little rule which one notes with interest. She would not allow the gentlemen to remain over their after-dinner wine more than a quarter of an hour, and always remained standing in the drawing-room until they made their appearance. The evening was spent in music and conversation, varied by quadrille parties; the Duchess of Kent always having her rubber of whist. At half-past eleven the Queen retired. Her life at Windsor was varied by sojourns at Buckingham Palace and at the Pavilion at Brighton. Wherever she was, each hour of the day was mapped out, and she spent no idle moments, having the happy faculty for working when she worked and playing when she played. If the Queen had led a quiet, uneventful girlhood, she certainly made up for lost time now, and there was no one in Her Majesty's dominions who enjoyed life with its pleasures and gaieties more thoroughly.

    And so the months passed swiftly by until in the merry month of June all the town was agog for the Coronation. Country cousins came flocking in by the thousand. Every hotel and lodging-house was filled from garret to basement, and there was not a private house without staying-guests. It was calculated that there were some five hundred thousand people from the provinces in London, in addition to the distinguished representatives from every court in Europe, with their retinues. On the morning of the 28th, at seventeen minutes past three, just as the first streak of dawn appeared in the horizon, a salute of twenty-one guns heralded in the auspicious day, and from every tower and steeple rang out a joyous peal. The hundreds and thousands of the poorer folk who had passed the night in the streets looked anxiously at some ominous dark clouds in the sky, but after a slight shower they dispersed, and the sun shone bright and gloriously.

    At five o'clock the doors of Westminster Abbey were thrown open to the eager crowd of ticket-holders, and the bells of St. Margaret's clanged and pealed.

    At length the firing of the Park guns announced that the royal procession had left the Palace. At the boisterous salute the young Queen put her hands to her ears in mock alarm, and then chatted merrily with the Duchess of Sutherland, who, as Mistress of the Robes, rode in the carriage with her. The Queen wore a dress of crimson velvet and ermine richly adorned with diamonds and pearls. On her head was a gold circlet fixed on to a cap of purple velvet lined with white taffeta and turned up with ermine. Eight lovely girls of the highest nobility, dressed in white silk, with blush-roses, attended like a bevy of fairy nymphs to bear her train.

Her Majesty's State carriage was drawn by eight cream-coloured horses, and the equipages of the foreign ambassadors were in corresponding magnificence. For length and picturesque effect no such procession had ever passed along the streets of London. The "old folks" about her had endeavoured to persuade the young Queen not to have a public procession; but while she willingly renounced the time-honoured banquet at Westminster Hall, she insisted upon coming out amongst her people, and chose the most circuitous route to the Abbey. Once the traces of her carriage broke, and she sat with perfect composure while the damage was repaired; and when at another point the crowd pressed so closely that the equipage was brought to a standstill, she gave orders to wait awhile, and would not allow her guards to use violence to the people. This thoughtfulness had its reward. The coronation of the Maiden Monarch was a white day; not a single fatal accident marred its joyousness. The Duchess of Kent's carriage was stopped more than once by exuberant citizens, who insisted upon shaking hands with her as a token of approval of the manner in which she had reared their Queen. Marshal Soult came in for vociferous cheering, and Waterloo was forgotten as he and the Duke of Wellington shook hands.

An eye-witness relates that the Queen entered the Abbey "gay as a lark and looking like a girl on her birthday." A moment of breathless silence preceded her entry; then from choir and organ burst forth the strains of the anthem, "I was glad when they said unto me, Let us go into the house of the Lord," as, with her brilliant following, she swept slowly along to the centre of the choir. The anthem now gave place to a thrilling rendering of "God Save the Queen," with trumpet accompaniment. The cannon boomed, but the sound was deadened by the tumultuous acclamations within the Abbey as the Queen reached the Recognition Chair, beside the altar. She knelt a few moments in silent prayer. When she arose, the Westminster boys seized the golden opportunity, and, rising en masse, shouted with one voice, "Victoria, Victoria! Vivat Victoria Regina!"

The Archbishop now presented the Queen to the people in the quaint formula, "Sirs, I here present unto you Queen Victoria, the undoubted Queen of this realm; wherefore, all you who are come this day to do your homage, are you willing to do the same?" which was answered from all points of the compass, as Her Majesty turned to the north, to the south, to the east, and to the west, by "Long Live Queen Victoria," accompanied by the blowing of trumpets and the waving of banners.

The Coronation, with its various ceremonies, civil and religious, lasted more than four hours, and throughout the Queen played her part with wonderful composure. Care had been taken to provide a crown suitable for her small head; but no one had thought about reducing the size of the orb which she was required to carry in her tiny hand. "What am I to do with it?" she asked in concern. "Carry it, your Majesty," replied Lord John Thynne. "Am I? It is very heavy," the Queen answered in a tone of amazement. However, it was too late for protest, and she obeyed the exigencies of the situation. A worse mistake had been made with regard to the ruby coronation-ring. The jeweller had made it to fit Her Majesty's little finger, whereas the Archbishop declared that according to the rubric it must be put upon the larger finger, and accordingly forced it into that position. The Queen bore her painfully swelling finger with the same heroism that she carried the weighty orb. Afterwards the ringer was so much swollen that it had to be bathed in iced water before the ring could be drawn off.

The supreme moment of the ceremony came when the crown was placed upon the Queen's head. At the same instant the peers and peeresses put on their coronets, the bishops their mitres, the heralds their caps, whilst the trumpets sounded, the drums beat, the cannon outside fired, the Tower guns answered, and the people within and without rent the air with shouts of "God Save the Queen!" After this came the ceremony of the Homage, when all the Lords spiritual and temporal ascended the steps of the throne, and, taking off their coronets, touched the crown on the Queen's head, repeated the quaint oath of allegiance, and kissed her hand. Formerly it had been the cheek of the monarch which was kissed. During the Homage occurred the episode of old Lord Rolle, who was so infirm that his effort to ascend the steps to the throne resulted in his falling down, but such was his loyalty that he again essayed the impossible feat. Then it was that the Queen rose from the throne and held out her hand to the old man, pityingly as a daughter might have done. An old lady, who was present at the Coronation and often described the scene to the present writer, when she came to this part of the story used to lose all control of the aspirates in her excitement, and invariably finished the narration with: "And then, my dear, when the sweet young Queen rose from her throne, and extended her hand for that gouty old lord to kiss, I thought that the Abbey would have come down with the cheering."

It was four o'clock in the afternoon before the Queen entered the State coach for the return journey. All the way back to the Palace she smiled and bowed to the exultant crowds, performing her part beautifully to the last, although the strain of the day's work would have prostrated most young ladies. On entering the Palace court and hearing the bark of her favourite dog, she exclaimed, "There's Dash; I must go and give him his bath." It is easy to imagine with what a sense of relief the young Queen put off her State trappings, the ring which had caused her such discomfort, and the heavy orb which had made her wrist ache, to have a frolic with her pet and a brief rest before she received the one hundred guests who composed her dinner-party that evening. For several days revelry reigned throughout London, and indeed in every place in the country. The poor were feasted, the school-children had holiday, and business was forgotten in one loyal burst of enthusiasm. The most noticeable feature in the metropolis was the great Coronation Fair in Hyde Park, lasting for four days, which the Queen honoured with her presence.

BETROTHAL AND EARLY MARRIED LIFE OF QUEEN VICTORIA

WHEN Queen Victoria announced to her Prime Minister that she had resolved to marry, Lord Melbourne replied, with paternal solicitude: "Your Majesty will be much more comfortable, for a woman cannot stand alone for any time, in whatever position she may be."

This was in the autumn of 1839, and the previous six months had probably been to the young Queen the most unhappy which she had ever experienced, owing to the strifes and jealousies of the two great political parties in the country. The atmosphere of reserve in which Her Majesty was compelled to live was very unnatural for a young girl, and oppressive to one of her open, candid disposition. Often she must have longed for the companionship of one with whom she could be herself, unrestricted by regal considerations. The happy change which her marriage wrought in her isolated position is thus expressed by the Queen: "We must all have trials and vexations; but if one's home is happy, then the rest is comparatively nothing.... My happiness at home, the love of my husband, his kindness, his advice, his support, and his company make up for all."

There were many suitors for the hand of the fair occupant of the greatest throne in the world, among them the Prince of Orange; and it is a curious coincidence that a former Prince of Orange came a-wooing to the Princess Charlotte. After a period of indecision, that royal lady dismissed her suitor peremptorily, not, however, without going to the window to take a last look at him as he mounted his horse, which caused the ladies-in-waiting to think that the Princess was about to relent; but when, after gazing intently at his retreating figure, clad in a scarlet uniform surmounted by a hat with nodding green plumes, she exclaimed, "How like a radish he looks!" it was felt that his fate was finally settled. There are not any stories about Queen

Victoria either receiving or dismissing suitors, the proposals for her hand being made officially and rejected in the same manner. The one love episode of her life was with her cousin, Prince Albert, second son of the reigning Duke of Saxe-Coburg-Gotha, and all the world knows of its happy fulfilment.

When a small boy, Prince Albert was often promised by his nurse, as a reward for good behaviour, that he should marry his cousin, the Princess Victoria. Such a union had been designed by fond relatives when the children were yet in their cradles, and became the darling hope of Grandmamma of Coburg and Uncle Leopold, and was favoured by the Queen's mother, the Duchess of Kent, though it was by no means popular with King William IV. and the royal dukes. A visit was paid by Prince Albert to the Duchess of Kent, at Kensington Palace, in 1836, and he then made a favourable impression upon the Princess Victoria. The cousins rode, sang, played, danced, and walked together, and enjoyed each other's society after the usual manner of a youth and maiden at the impressionable age of seventeen. We have heard of little love tokens exchanged, but it is not generally known that a ring — a small enamel with a tiny diamond in the centre — was given by the Prince to his pretty cousin during this visit. This early gift from her lover has always been worn by the Queen, together with her engagement-ring, a beautiful emerald serpent, above her wedding-ring, which, we believe, has never been taken off since her wedding-day. One of her ladies tells the story that, when a sculptor was modelling Her Majesty's hand, she was in an agony lest the ring should come off with the plaster, which she would have regarded as a bad omen.

After the return of the Prince to Germany, letters occasionally passed between him and the Princess Victoria; but after her accession to the throne even these cousinly epistles ceased. In reply to the wish expressed by her Uncle Leopold that a formal betrothal with Prince Albert should take place, the young Queen said that she wished the affair to be considered as broken off, and that for four years she could not think of marriage. Not that her feelings towards the Prince had really changed, for Her Majesty says that, "from her girlhood, she had never thought of marrying any one else." It was the Prince's youth which stood in the way. Girl though she was, the Queen had plenty of sound common sense, and she shrewdly suspected that, though the people were romantically loyal to a young maiden, their lawful sovereign, they might not be very enthusiastic about a consort who was only a youth of eighteen. Moreover, the Queen had her part to learn, for she had determined to be a ruling monarch, and it seemed better that she should be unfettered by new ties during her apprenticeship in statecraft. In short, Her Majesty found queenhood enough for the present, without the addition of wifehood and motherhood.

But when, in after years, she realised the burden of a crown, and the value of the wise head beside her own, and the comfort of a loving husband's help, she greatly regretted that her marriage had not taken place earlier, and with characteristic candour Her Majesty has expressed the indignation which she feels against herself at having kept the Prince waiting. The excuse which the Queen makes is that the sudden change from the secluded life at Kensington to the independence of her position as Queen Regnant, at the age of eighteen, put all ideas of marriage out of her mind. "A worse school for a young girl," she adds, "or one more detrimental to all natural feelings and affections, cannot well be imagined, than the position of a queen at eighteen, without experience and without a husband to guide and support her. This the Queen can state from painful experience, and she thanks God that none of her dear daughters are exposed to such danger."

It was a few months after her coronation that the Queen realised the words, "Uneasy lies the head that wears a crown." Party jealousy now began to make her its victim, the Tories growing jealous of the Whig influences which surrounded the sovereign. The Queen's father had been a staunch Whig; her mother sympathised with his views, as did also her uncle, King Leopold; the Whigs were in power at the time of the Queen's accession, and her chief friend, adviser, and political tutor was the Prime Minister, Lord Melbourne. It was said that the Tories, in order to destroy the Whig influences about the Queen, plotted the fall of Melbourne by hatching a Court scandal. There was in attendance upon the Duchess of Kent a beautiful and accomplished woman, the Lady Flora Hastings, and rumours were set afloat that the behaviour of this lady was such as to render her continuance about the person of the Queen's mother a scandal. Things were represented to Her Majesty in such a light as to leave her no option but to banish Lady Flora from Court. The Marchioness of Hastings then demanded an investigation into the charges made, which resulted in the complete vindication of her daughter's character. Lady Flora, in writing an account of the affair to an uncle in Brussels, states that the Duchess of Kent treated her with great tenderness after the explosion of the scandal, and that the Queen expressed her regret "handsomely, with tears in her eyes." However, a few months later the unfortunate lady died. It was alleged by many that Lady Flora had died of a broken heart, and scurrilous letters were addressed to the Queen's private secretary and confidante, the Baroness Lehzen, accusing her of having plotted the downfall of Lady Flora. Capital was made out of the affair by the Tories, and it was argued that Lord Melbourne was responsible for having allowed such a scandal to creep into the Court of the young Queen. Shortly afterwards, upon a narrow Government majority, Lord Melbourne resigned office.

Her Majesty was in the greatest grief, both concerning the case of Lady Flora Hastings and at the resignation of the Melbourne Ministry. She kept her private apartments for a day, and was in deep sorrow. To part with the Prime Minister seemed like losing her only friend and adviser; still, she must face the exigencies of her position, and accordingly the news went through the town that "the Queen had sent for the Duke." In the popular mind of those days England had but one Duke, and that was the hero of Waterloo. Wellington, however, declined to form a ministry, and the Queen on his advice sent for Sir Robert Peel. Her Majesty was naively frank with Sir Robert, and told him that it was a grief to her to part with her late Government; still, she was prepared to do her duty as a monarch. All went well until it was intimated that the Ladies of the Royal Household must be replaced by others favourable to the party now in power; then the woman arose within her, and the Queen distinctly refused to part with her loved and valued friends, foremost among whom was the Mistress of the Robes, the beautiful Duchess of Sutherland, for whose splendid qualities the Queen had the greatest admiration. The Duchess was a daughter of the noble Howard family, and the wife of a Scotch duke. Her interests in the literary and philanthropic movements of the day, and in all that affected the well-being and advancement of women, are well known, and while she reigned at Stafford House it was a centre of the forward social movements of the day. It was in her drawing-room that Harriet Beecher-Stowe pleaded the cause of the slave. We do not wonder that the Queen did not like losing the attendance of such a truly noble Duchess, nor of Lady Normanby, the Duchess of Bedford, and the other ladies; but it was, we believe, unconstitutional for her to refuse the wishes of her Ministers. Writing of the affair to Lord Melbourne she said: "They wanted to deprive me of my Ladies; and I suppose they would deprive me next of my dressers and housemaids; they wished to treat me like a girl, but I will show them that I am Queen of England." And she did too, for the combined efforts of the Duke of Wellington and Sir Robert Peel could get no further concession from Her Majesty than, "You may take my Lords, but not my Ladies."

Her Majesty was beginning to find that standing alone was not a very pleasant thing, and when, in the autumn of 1839, Prince Albert, accompanied by his brother, Prince Ernest, paid a visit to Windsor Castle, her views about marrying underwent a change. The Prince was now greatly improved by foreign travel, and had developed into a strikingly handsome man, with graceful, winning manners. A graphic sketch of Prince Albert at this period was written by an English gentleman resident at Gotha: "His Serene Highness Prince Albert is a fine young man; his complexion is clear; his eyes greyish blue, exceedingly expressive; his features are regular, the forehead expanding nobly, and giving the notion of intellectual power. His hair is brown, parted on the side of the head in the modern fashion. He wears mustachios, which add much to the manliness of his countenance, and he has also whiskers. He is exceedingly erect in his person, and is said to excel in all the martial exercises of the military profession, and to be exceedingly au fait in the more elegant exercises of the drawing-room, the saloon, and the ball-room." He was three months younger than the Queen, having been born August, 1819, at Rosenau, the summer residence of his father, the reigning Duke of Saxe-Coburg-Gotha. An unhappy estrangement took place between his parents when he was a little fellow of five, and he never again saw the beautiful mother whom he was said to resemble, and for whose memory he entertained the deepest affection. She died murmuring the names "Ernest!" "Albert!" — the two boys, whom in her last moments she longed to clasp in her arms. The young Princes were carefully trained by their father, and watched with loving solicitude by their two grandmothers. Prince Albert pursued his studies at the University of Bonn, and became an accomplished student in literature and the fine arts. He was thoughtful, reserved, and dignified beyond his years, and a veritable Galahad in all the moral virtues; it seemed to every one that he was just the man to make the young Queen happy.

When the Prince came to Windsor in 1839, he was undoubtedly a little touched in his dignity, and had resolved to tell the Queen, like a man, that he was not going to be played with; she must make up her mind to a formal betrothal or consider the affair at an end. His mind, however, was soon set at rest. "On the second day after our arrival," he wrote home to a college friend, "the most friendly demonstrations were directed towards me, and two days later I was secretly called to a private audience, in which the Queen offered me her hand and heart. I think," he adds, "that I shall be very happy, for Victoria possesses all the qualities which make a home happy, and seems to be attached to me with her whole heart."

Her Majesty's superior rank made it imperative that the proposal of marriage should come from her, and it is variously reported how she made it. There is a story that she tentatively asked the Prince such leading questions as, "How did he like England?" "Would he like to make it his home?" But the Prince says that the Queen declared her feeling for him in a "genuine outburst of love and affection," with which he was "quite enchanted and carried away." The proposal was made on the morning of the 15th of October, 1839. The Prince had been out hunting early with his brother, and immediately after his return the Queen summoned him to her boudoir and made the interesting communication. The happiness of the young pair seems to have been beyond expression, and we find both of them writing ecstatic letters to their near relations; the Queen dwelling upon the great sacrifice which the Prince was making in leaving his country to share her life, and he in his turn feeling all unworthy of the love which was shown him. Uncle Leopold and the worthy Baron Stockmar were delighted at the news, and both the Duchess of Kent and Lord Melbourne were pleased also. Beyond these and a favoured few the engagement was not made known until after Prince Albert had returned home.

For a whole month the lovers courted in secret. The Queen took her first holiday from Lord Melbourne's political instructions, and enjoyed a merry time, galloping about the Park in the day with the handsome Prince at her side, and having delightful little dances and festivities in the evening. She reviewed the troops in the Home Park, dressed in her Windsor uniform and cap, and mounted on her old charger "Leopold," having the Prince in his green uniform of the Coburg troops on her right hand. It rained and was piercingly cold, but what did that matter when "dearest Albert" settled her cape "so comfortably" for her?

The gay, happy time came to an end all too soon. The Prince and his brother returned home, and the Queen, according to the gossip of the time, gave herself up to a sweet melancholy, and would sing only German songs; and in sympathy with the royal lovers young ladies warbled "I caught her tear at parting," which became the popular song of the day. The royal lovers corresponded daily, and the miscarriage of one of the letters was the occasion of an amusing incident. The Queen was sitting one morning at Windsor Castle in conversation with Lord Melbourne, when word was brought that a young man had called demanding to see the Queen on private business. Her Majesty of course declined to see the stranger; but finding that he would not go away unheard, Lord Melbourne went to inquire what he wanted. He refused to say at first, but, further pressed, admitted that he had a packet which he must place in no one's hands but those of the Queen. Finally he was brought to the royal presence, and drawing forth from his breast a mysterious package he delivered it to Her Majesty, who on opening it found that it was a letter from Prince Albert, which had been omitted by mistake from the royal letter-bag, and which the postal authorities had sent by special messenger. The young man received a suitable reward, and was commended for his fidelity to his trust.

In the midst of her new-found happiness the Queen had important business to perform; first the Privy Council was summoned, and she declared to these solemn old gentlemen, some eighty in number, that it was her intention to marry Prince Albert of Saxe-Coburg and Gotha. The reading of the formal declaration only occupied a few minutes, and Her Majesty says that she was very nervous, and saw nothing save Lord Melbourne looking at her with tears in his eyes, and upon her wrist the medallion of her "beloved Albert," which seemed to give her courage. Next came a more trying ordeal still, the announcement of her approaching marriage in a speech from the throne, in the House of Lords. She did it with the utmost dignity, and in those clear musical tones so peculiar to her. Both were doubtless "nervous occasions," but the Queen confided to the Duchess of Gloucester that neither of them was half so trying as "having to propose to Albert." The troubles were not as yet over, and it seemed that the course of true love was not in this case to run smooth. There was heated discussion both in and out of Parliament regarding the allowance to be given to the Prince. The original proposal of £50,000 a year was voted down to £30,000, and the discussion concerning it was in the worst possible taste; when Mr. Hume told Lord John Russell that he "must know the danger of setting a young man down in London with so much money in his pockets," the House, instead of calling him to order, roared with laughter. Then came the matter of the Prince's precedency. The Queen wished a clause put in the Naturalisation Bill to the effect that her husband was to take rank in the country next to herself, but the royal Dukes, her uncles, objected to this, and Parliament dropped the clause, upon which the Queen asserted her royal prerogative that it was her will and pleasure that the Prince should "enjoy place, pre-eminence, and precedence next to Her Majesty." This settled the question within British dominions; but the refusal of Parliament to pass the Precedency Clause left it optional with foreign courts to give the Prince the same royal status as his wife, and in after years caused the Queen great annoyance when visiting continental sovereigns. The Queen's sentiments were very creditable to her womanly feelings, and we do not wonder that she was highly indignant at the action of Parliament, for was not the Prince to be regarded, not only as the Queen's husband, but as the father of our kings to be? The nation practically insulted itself when it refused him royal status.

With manly independence Prince Albert refused all the titles which his future wife might have conferred upon him, and never displayed the least resentment at the recent squabbles over his income and precedence. "While I possess your love," he wrote to the Queen, "they cannot make me unhappy."

The Queen's wedding was a grand and beautiful pageant. It took place on the 10th of February, 1840, in the Royal Chapel of St. James, before an assembly second only in magnificence to that which had witnessed her coronation in Westminster Abbey. The royal bride was pale, but looked very sweet in her magnificent bridal robe of Honiton lace over white satin trimmed with the time-honoured orange blossoms. The train was of white satin trimmed with the same flowers, and borne by two pages of honour. Her veil was comparatively short, being only one yard and a half square, and was worn flowing back from the wreath over her shoulders, leaving her face uncovered. She wore a necklace and earrings of diamonds, and the armlet of the Garter. The satin for the dress was manufactured at Spitalfields, and the Honiton lace was made by two hundred poor lace-workers in the village of Beer, near to Honiton, the Queen sending Miss Bidney from London to superintend the work. The joy of these poor women at being employed, expressly by the Queen's command, to make her bridal lace was unbounded; they could not sufficiently express their gratitude. When the lace was completed, the pattern was destroyed.

The wedding took place from Buckingham Palace at noon. Previously royal marriages had been celebrated in an evening, but it was the wish of the Queen to conform to the same rule as her subjects, and she was also desirous of giving them an opportunity to see the procession as it passed to the Chapel Royal. First down the grand staircase of the Palace came the bridegroom, looking very handsome in his uniform with the collar of the Garter, surmounted by two white rosettes, carrying a Prayer Book bound in green velvet in his hand. He was accompanied by his father, the Duke of Saxe-Coburg and his brother, Prince Ernest, and as he passed to his carriage was saluted by the household with the same honours given to royal personages. When he entered the chapel, the organ played "See the Conquering Hero Comes." He was the man who among all the princes of Europe had secured Victoria, Queen of England, for his bride. After an interval Her Majesty the Queen, escorted by her Lord Chamberlain, came sweeping slowly down the grand staircase in her snowy satin and lace, graciously acknowledging the obeisances made and looking very lovely. It was observed that for this occasion she had laid aside her crown, and only a wreath of orange blossoms rested upon her brow. She was accompanied by Her Royal Highness the Duchess of Kent, wearing a white satin dress embroidered in silver, and by the Duchess of Sutherland, Mistress of the Robes, who wore a superb dress of pink moiré, embroidered in sea-weed and shell pattern At the Chapel Royal twelve bridesmaids, young and fair, dressed in white, with wreaths of pale roses, were ready to attend her to the altar. She was given away by her uncle of Sussex, of whom a wag of the time said, "The Duke of Sussex is always ready to give away what does not belong to him."

The marriage service was conducted according to the rubric of the Church of England, the Archbishop having dutifully waited upon Her Majesty beforehand, to know if the promise "to obey" was to be omitted, but she replied that she wished "to be married as a woman, not as Queen." When Prince Albert solemnly repeated the words, "With all my worldly goods I thee endow," it was observed by some that the bride gave him an arch smile. He took the wedding-ring from his own finger to hand it to the

Archbishop, and when it was placed upon the Queen's slender finger volleys of cannon mingled with the pealing and the clanging of the marriage bells. Unfortunately "Queen's weather," which has since become proverbial, did not prevail; but the rain did not damp the loyalty of the people, and the streets were thronged with cheering multitudes to greet the young Queen and the husband of her choice. As Prince Albert led his wife from the altar he held her hand in a position which prominently displayed the wedding-ring. It is said that the Queen's look of confidence and comfort at the Prince as they walked away together as man and wife was very pleasing to see. It was such a new thing for her to have an equal companion, friend, and husband, a young heart against which she could rest her own. Few bridegrooms show to advantage at the wedding ceremony; but the quiet dignity and stately simplicity of bearing shown by the Prince filled every one with admiration. After the marriage register had been signed in the royal attestation book, placed upon a golden table, the wedding party returned to Buckingham Palace to a dejeuner. The great feature of the table was the gigantic wedding cake — three hundred pounds in weight, three yards in circumference, and fourteen inches in depth, which took four men to carry it. The ornamentation was superb. On the top was Britannia blessing the royal couple, and amongst other figures was a cupid writing in a volume spread upon his knees, "10th February, 1840."

The brief honeymoon of three days was spent at Royal Windsor, where the Prince was seen driving his wife about, tete-a-tete, in a pony phaeton. The day after her marriage the Queen wrote to Baron Stockmar, "There cannot exist a purer, dearer, nobler being in the world than the Prince." Happy Queen! that in the years which followed she never had occasion to modify her young bride's enthusiasm. A Royal Idyll had indeed begun such as this country had never looked upon before.

As a memento of the occasion Her Majesty presented each of the officiating clergy with a handsomely bound volume containing a suitable inscription, and to each of the bridesmaids she gave a brooch in the form of a bird, the body being formed of turquoises, the eyes of rubies, the beak of a diamond, the claws of pure gold, resting upon pearls of great size and value. In accordance also with an early English custom, she ordered a number of wedding-rings to be made, with her portrait engraved in the centre and surrounded by true lovers' knots, to send as gifts to her special friends. We wonder that this pretty custom of olden times has not had a modern revival.

On the 14th of February the Queen and the Prince returned with the Court to Buckingham Palace, the roads along the route being lined with enthusiastic crowds exhibiting white favours. Next day Her Majesty held a levee, and was conducted to her seat by her husband, who took his stand beside her, a position which he ever afterwards retained at all State functions. When in the autumn the Queen prorogued Parliament in person, the Prince accompanied her, and sat on the seat of honour beside the throne. By this act Her Majesty settled the question of her husband's precedency, and the Duke of Wellington said afterwards, with an inward chuckle: "I told you that was the best way to settle the dispute — let the Queen place the Prince where she thinks fit." My lords and gentlemen were of course powerless to oppose the action of a young bride, and a Queen to boot, who would insist upon having her husband at her side.

In the height of the brilliant season which succeeded the royal marriage, London was startled on the evening of the 10th of June by the report of the attempted assassination of the Queen. She was driving with Prince Albert up Constitution Hill when a young man named Oxford presented a pistol and fired directly at her. The Prince rose in consternation to shield his wife, and meantime the miscreant fired again, and was this time seized by the bystanders. Her Majesty displayed the utmost courage, rising in her seat to show the people that she was not hurt, and then ordered her postilions to drive to Ingestre House, where the Duchess of Kent was now living, her first thought being to save her mother the shock of an exaggerated report. Old people still speak of the unbounded demonstrations of loyalty which the affair occasioned, and of the gay cavalcade of ladies and gentlemen which for days afterwards attended the Queen's carriage as a voluntary bodyguard when she drove in the Park. Two days later Her Majesty visited the opera, and received an unparalleled ovation of loyalty, and, what pleased her best of all, the Prince was called for and given three separate cheers. Previous to this Prince Albert had presided at a great public meeting in Exeter Hall for the Abolition of the Slave Trade, and made an excellent speech in English, which he had rehearsed to the Queen in the morning. One can imagine how proud she was that his first public effort was in so good a cause, for it was one which had been of deep interest to her since those early days when she had listened to slave stories from the lips of Wilberforce on the Ramsgate sands. The sweet Quakeress, Caroline Fox, was there to beam approval upon the Prince, whom she thought "a very beautiful young man."

Society was soon thrown into a state of interested expectancy, as the journals spoke of the Queen as looking less blooming than usual, and the last Drawing-Room of the season was held by Her Majesty sitting; her dainty white-slippered feet resting on a gold brocaded cushion. Early in November elaborate preparations were made at Buckingham Palace for the approaching accouchement of the Queen, and there on the 21st of the month at 1.40 p.m. a little Princess Royal was born. The Prince was a little disappointed that it was a girl; but the Queen said, "Never mind, the next one shall be a boy," adding the hope that she might have as many children as her grandmother, Queen Charlotte. The next day there was a scare in the Palace by reason of the discovery of a disreputable little urchin, known to fame as "the boy Jones," under a sofa in a room next to that of the Queen. He audaciously acknowledged to having listened with interest to Her Majesty conversing with Prince Albert. Being too young for punishment he was sent to a House of Correction.

The devotion of Prince Albert during his wife's seclusion was an example to all husbands. The Queen has recorded that he was content to sit by her side in a darkened room, to read to her and write for her. No one but himself ever lifted her from her bed to the sofa, and he always helped to wheel her on her bed or sofa into the next room. For this purpose he would come instantly from any part of the house. His care for her was like that of a mother; "nor could there," adds the Queen, "be a kinder or more judicious nurse." A month after her confinement Her Majesty was keeping Christmas at Windsor in right merry style, and a Christmas tree was set up to please the baby, and there were trees also for the Household — a pretty custom first introduced into this country by Prince Albert. The stately Castle had never witnessed such homely gaiety in royal personages before. On the 10th of February, the first anniversary of the Wedding Day, the Princess Royal received her mother's name, and several others besides, with befitting ceremonial in the throne-room of Buckingham Palace. In the following November, on Lord Mayor's Day, the Queen was as good as her word, and presented her husband with a son, and the nation with a Prince of Wales.

The following amusing incident, in connection with the framing of the bulletin announcing the royal birth, occurred. After the usual statement the bulletin ran thus: "Her Majesty and the Prince are perfectly well." When this was shown to the Queen by Prince Albert, previous to its publication, she said, with a laugh, "My dear, this will never do." "Why not?" asked the Prince. "Because," replied the Queen, "it conveys the idea that you were confined also." Prince Albert was a little dumbfounded, but the bulletin was altered to, "Her Majesty and the infant Prince are perfectly well."

There was another merry Christmas at Windsor, and this year there were two pairs of little eyes to view the Christmas tree. The christening of the heir to the throne was a very imposing ceremony, and took place on the 25th of January, 1842, in St. George's Chapel, Windsor. The King of Prussia came to stand as chief sponsor. The infant Prince was named Albert after his father, and Edward after his grandfather, the Duke of Kent. At the conclusion of the ceremony the overjoyed father requested that the Hallelujah Chorus might be sung. Immediately afterwards the Queen held a chapter of the Order of the Garter, and appointed the illustrious godfather a Knight Companion, herself buckling the Garter round his knee.

The year 1842 was a memorable one in the Queen's life for many things. In June she took her first trip by rail, returning from Windsor by the Great Western Railway to Paddington, the famous engineer, Brunei, driving the engine. There was a royal saloon provided, and crimson carpets were laid from the Queen's carriage to the train. The journey occupied twenty-five minutes, and Her Majesty was received by a large assembly, with great applause, when she reached the terminus, although wiseacres probably shook their heads and wondered that the royal lady had not more sense than to trust herself to such an infernal machine. In this year two attempts were made upon the Queen's life; the first by John Francis, who fired a pistol at her when she was driving down Constitution Hill. It appears that he had held a pistol in a threatening attitude the day before, and the Queen, with her usual bravery, determined to drive out again and let him do his worst, rather than have the uncertainty of another attack hanging over her. She would not allow her ladies to accompany her, which occasioned much surprise at the time; but, upon returning home, she said to Miss Liddell, one of the maids of honour: "I dare say, Georgy, you were surprised at not driving with me this afternoon, but the fact was that, as we returned from church yesterday, a man presented a pistol at the carriage window, which flashed in the pan; we were so taken by surprise that he had time to escape; so I knew what was hanging over me, and I was determined to expose no life but my own." Francis was tried and sentenced to death, but was reprieved at the Queen's request. The next attempt on her life was made by a hunchback, John Bean, who levelled a pistol at Her Majesty when she was driving to the Chapel Royal; fortunately it did not go off. The London season of 1842 was marked by two functions of great splendour. First came what was called at the time the Queen's Masque; though it has descended into history as the Plantagenet Ball. The entertainment took place at Buckingham Palace, and was a magnificent historical picture arranged and planned by Her Majesty. The chief feature was the assemblage and meeting of the Courts of Edward and Philippa with Anne of Brittany, after which quadrilles were danced by representatives of all nationalities, succeeded by a general dance in which all were blended. In the Highland set the present Duke of Argyll, then the young Marquis of Lorne, took a spirited part. Her Majesty, as Queen Philippa, wore a magnificent dress of the period in blue and gold brocade trimmed with fur, and having a stomacher literally blazing with jewels, the cost of which was estimated at £60,000. It was on view in Hanover Square previous to the day of the ball, and two hundred and fifty carriages stood at one time crowded with ladies waiting their turn to get a sight of the lovely and magnificent robe. A fortnight later came the famous ball held at Covent Garden for the relief of the Spitalfields weavers, which was attended by the Queen and Prince Albert in state. These and other minor festivities which followed were planned by the Queen with a view to stimulating trade; but her motives were misunderstood and much called in question at the time, and there were papers which printed the cost of the Court pageants in one column, and gave the list of those who were dying from starvation in another.

In the autumn of 1842 the Queen paid her first visit to Scotland, accompanied by the Prince. She travelled by water, and was received at Granton Pier by the Duke of Buccleuch, driving through Edinburgh to Dalkeith Palace. The new experiences of the first visit paid outside her native land delighted the Queen, and found very graphic expression in her Highland Journal. Nothing escaped her quick eyes; the many-storied houses of the Old Town, the aged crones standing at the doors in their white mutches, the bare-footed lads and lassies, the fish-wives in their short petticoats, with the "caller herrin', fresh drawn frae the Forth" in kreels upon their backs, and all the sights of the historic town were quickly noted down. Her Majesty took oatmeal porridge to her breakfast, tried the "Finnan haddies," and pronounced the homely Scottish fare excellent. She held a reception at Holyrood Palace, and a levee at Dalkeith House, visited Lord Rosebery (grandfather of the present Earl) at Dalmeny, and journeyed farther north to the Highlands, visiting all the places of interest en route. Scott was constantly in her hand, and she delighted to verify the places and scenes of which he wrote. Never probably had the Queen so enjoyed a holiday. She roamed about the lochs and glens, made friends with the old women in the cottages, and enjoyed a freedom which was absolutely new to her. Great was her amusement to see the astonishment of one old woman, when told that the young lady to whom she had given flowers from her garden was the Queen. The ancient dame rubbed up her best English, and endeavoured to make Her Majesty understand that she was right welcome to Scotland. There were torchlight dances, and reels and strathspeys for the entertainment of the royal visitors, with all of which the Queen was greatly pleased, and at the close of the tour she confessed to having become quite fond of hearing the bagpipes.

Everywhere she was received with enthusiasm, and many are the stories told of the criticisms, full of pawky humour, offered by the crowd. A gentleman in Edinburgh said to his farm-servant, "Well, John, did you see the Queen?" "Troth did I that, sir. I was terrible 'feared afore she came forrit — my heart was maist in my mouth, but when she did come forrit, I was na feared at a'; I just lookit at her, and she lookit at me, an' she bowed her heid at me, an' I bowed my heid at her. She's a raal fine leddie, wi'oot a bit o' pride aboot her at a'." The Queen quitted Scotland on the 15th of September, after staying a fortnight. "As the fair shores of Scotland receded more and more from our view," she writes in her journal, "we felt quite sad that this very pleasant and interesting tour was over; but we shall never forget it."

After their return home, the Queen and the Prince took their two little children on a visit to the Duke of Wellington at Walmer Castle, to get the sea air. The following spring sweet little Princess Alice was added to the royal nursery, and the Queen was now beginning to feel great responsibility about the training and education of her rapidly increasing family. "It is hard," she once said, "that I cannot always hear my children say their prayers." The duty of overlooking the management of the nursery, which the Queen would gladly have undertaken herself, if her position had permitted it, was delegated to Lady Lyttelton, one of the Ladies of the Bedchamber. The royal nursery became a very lively place, and many amusing stories are told by Lady Bloomfield, a lady-in-waiting, about the precocity of the Princess Royal. Whilst they were out driving one day, the Queen called her "Missy," which she often did. The Princess took no notice the first time; but the next she looked up very indignantly, and said to her mother, "I'm not Missy, I'm the Princess Royal." On another occasion, the Queen was talking to one of her ladies, and not taking any notice of the little Princess, who suddenly exclaimed: "There's a cat under the trees" — fertile imagination on her part — but, having succeeded in drawing attention, she quietly said: "Cat come out to look at the Queen, I suppose."

And so the early married life of Queen Victoria glided peacefully by, rich in the love of husband and children; and though storms might threaten the political horizon, as yet there was no shadow on the home.

HOME AND COURT LIFE OF QUEEN VICTORIA

BY the year 1844 people were ceasing to speak of the "young Queen," for although Her Majesty was young in years, being only twenty-five, she was now a comely matron with four children — two boys and two girls — Prince Alfred having in this year succeeded little Princess Alice. It was to convey the tidings of Prince Alfred's birth from Windsor to London that the electric telegraph was first used to announce such an event.

The home life at Royal Windsor was, indeed, an example to the nation, and afforded the best object-lesson ever given as to the possibility of a woman combining public and political work with the duties of a wife and mother. We are indebted to a gentleman-at-arms for information regarding the Queen's mode of spending her day. Her Majesty rose at 6.30 in summer and 7.30 in winter. After making her toilet and attending morning service with the household, in the chapel, she breakfasted upon coffee, bread-and-butter, eggs or cold meat, then took a walk with her husband in the gardens and inspected the Home Farm. She was fond of seeing the poultry fed, and did not disdain to give the poor pigs a look. Then there were the aviary, studs, aquarium, and the pet animals to be visited; the favourite dogs bounded by her side with delight as she moved about, and the pigeons came out to perch on her shoulders and on Prince Albert's hat. Returning to the Castle, the royal mother inspected the nurseries and saw the older children at their studies; and having satisfied herself that everything was en regle, she glanced through the Times and Morning Post, after which she received the Master of the Household in the library, discussed the domestic arrangements for the day, received his report upon letters and applications addressed to her, and gave commands regarding the guests to be invited to the Castle. These usually arrived in time to dine, remained all next day, and returned home on the third, the three days being called days of "Rest," "Reception," and "Departure."

It may here be stated that in the first years of her married life the Queen made great alterations in the arrangement of the menage at Windsor. A Master of the Household was appointed to perform the duties which had hitherto belonged to three State officials, who were rarely on the premises to discharge their functions. So bad had been the regulations that if a pane of glass was broken in the scullery window, it took many weeks before the repair could be effected, owing to the difficulty of finding out whose duty it was to attend to it. A gentleman who had occasion to attend at the Castle related to the present writer that one morning he saw the Queen enter the dining-room and ring the bell several times before she could get any one to attend to her requirements. There was no one even to show guests to their bedrooms, which on one occasion led to an amusing incident. M. Guizot was a guest at the Palace, and upon retiring for the night he spent nearly an hour wandering about the corridors to try and identify his bedroom. At length he opened a door which he imagined led to it; but before he had advanced many steps into the room he discovered that a lady was seated before the toilet table with a maid brushing her hair. The abashed gentleman made a hasty retreat, and was fortunate when he returned to the bewildering corridors to find a guide who took him to his own room. The incident had almost passed from his mind, when the following evening he was reminded of it by a laughing allusion made by the Queen. M. Guizot then discovered that it was Her Majesty's dressing-room he had entered. Hitherto the unused bread had been wasted in the royal kitchens, but the Queen now directed that it should be sent to the inmates of the almshouses within the burgh of Windsor; and many other reforms were instituted by the royal housekeeper and her methodical husband.

But to return to her manner of portioning out her day. Having so far disposed of the household matters, the Queen turned her attention to affairs of State. At eleven o'clock the despatch boxes were opened, and their contents discussed with the principal secretaries of State, when necessary, or perused with the Prince. In the Foreign Secretary's box were all the recent correspondence with foreign powers and the drafts of the proposed replies for the Queen's consideration, and like minutiae were observed in the despatches of the War, Admiralty, and Home departments. After this business had been transacted, Her Majesty received visitors "invited" or "commanded" — artists, publishers, foreigners with special introductions, people with presents for the aviary, and tradesmen with novelties to exhibit. At two o'clock came luncheon, at which the Queen ate and drank heartily after her morning's work, and was ready to enjoy several hours' riding or driving in the afternoon, accompanied by the Prince, the Duchess of Kent, and often by one or other of the children. Whenever the Queen was staying at Windsor her mother occupied Frogmore House, quite near, and invariably dined with her daughter. On returning from driving the Queen and Prince spent some time in private. Sometimes they amused themselves with drawing etchings upon copper of their children or pet animals, which were printed at their private press. One of the most interesting of these was an etching by the Queen of the Princess Royal as a baby in long clothes, gazing at a parrot in a cage placed to arrest her attention. At one time Mr., afterwards Sir, George Hayter attended at Windsor Castle to give the Queen and the Prince instruction in etching.

Dinner, which took place at eight o'clock, was a stately affair, served by servants in scarlet and powder, while a military band played in an anteroom. The conversation took place in subdued whispers, except when the Queen addressed a guest. Politics were by her desire never discussed, and the gentlemen remained behind over their wine only for a very short time. An anecdote of the Queen's perfect courtesy as a hostess may here be mentioned. A certain nobleman, who was an abstainer, was dining with the Queen, and was asked by a royal Duchess present to drink wine with her. Upon his polite refusal the Duchess laughingly appealed to Her Majesty to use her authority over her water-drinking guest; but the Queen replied with a smile: "There is no compulsion at my table." Not infrequently she would have what one of her ladies termed a "tete-a-tete dinner," alone with her husband.

After the ceremonious dinner was over, the Queen chatted with the ladies and gentlemen in the drawing-room, unless there were special guests to claim her attention, in a charmingly free-and-easy manner. In her gay moods she was the life of the company, and we catch glimpses of her seizing hold of an astonished lady and whirling her round in a polka, or dancing a reel, a recent accomplishment which she had learned in the Highlands. Music played an important feature in the evening's entertainment, and the Queen would sing duets with her ladies, and did not disdain to act as accompanist. On one occasion Jenny Lind was singing before the Queen, and was put to considerable annoyance by the vagaries of the Court musician. Her Majesty's quick ear detected what was wrong, and advancing to the piano, she said, "I will accompany Miss Lind," which she did to perfection. Prince Albert also shared his wife's taste for music, and was a composer and an accomplished player upon the organ, which he considered the finest instrument for expressing the feelings. The prominent place given to music in the royal household exercised an immense influence over the life of the people, and these little impromptu concerts at Windsor Castle were the precursors of the musical evenings which became fashionable in society, and which gradually extended to the humbler homes of the land.

Mendelssohn was more than once an honoured guest at Windsor, and his letters give some charming accounts of the skill and enthusiasm of the Queen and Prince Albert in his own beloved art. The great composer thought very highly of the Queen's singing, more highly in fact than he deemed it good taste to admit in her presence; it was only after her Majesty's modest confession that she felt too nervous to take a long G properly, that Mendelssohn praised her heartily and with a clear conscience. It was owing to the efforts of the Queen and Prince Albert that the Castle band was brought to such perfection, and the wind largely superseded by stringed instruments. On one occasion, when some special music had to be practised, the bandmaster commanded a Sunday rehearsal, at which two German players, who were Methodists, refused to comply on conscientious grounds. The affair came to the Queen's ears, and she settled it immediately, saying, "I will have no more Sunday rehearsals."

And so we find the evenings at the Court being spent in music, little dances, conversation, and round games. "Patience" was a favourite game with the Prince, and Vingt-et-un was sometimes played, and "Follow my leader," and there was spinning of counters, asking of riddles, and playing tricks with stuffed mice — in short, a quiet evening at Windsor was very like an old-fashioned party in ordinary life, even to grandmamma having her rubber of whist. The Queen could get amusement out of very trifling things, and never seemed bored, or complained of ennui; the secret of it being that she was never idle. When one of her former maids of honour, then an ambassador's wife, told the Empress of Russia that she had received a letter from Queen Victoria, the Empress exclaimed, "What! in her own handwriting? Is it possible that the Queen finds time to write letters?"

Another trait in the Queen's character was her cheerfulness; in fact, when she started to laugh she found it difficult to stop, and her laugh was no company laugh, but thoroughly hearty. Mr. Gibson, R.A., tells a story that when Her Majesty was sitting to him, he asked permission to measure her mouth. "Oh, certainly," replied the Queen, "if I can only keep it still and not laugh." The proposal was so unexpected and droll that it was some time before the Queen could compose herself; directly she closed her mouth she burst out laughing again. The same sculptor describes a little conjugal episode which occurred when he was to model the Queen in evening dress. She came into the room accompanied by the Prince, who, like a fond young husband, had his arm round his wife's neck, and pointing to her shoulder said, "Mr. Gibson, you must give me this dimple." Her Majesty's neck and shoulders were greatly admired in those days.

Now and again amusing celebrities were commanded to Windsor, notably Tom Thumb, who strutted about like a little peacock, and told the

Queen, to her amusement, that her place was "first rate." Charles Kean acted as Her Majesty's Master oi the Revels, and under his superintendence her friends the "poor players" gave many celebrated performances at the Castle. In those days the "boards" were trod by Macready, Phelps, and the Kembles, and Rachel and Grisi were the stars of the operatic stage. It was the Queen who first invited Jenny Lind to sing in this country, she having heard her in Coburg in '45, and when "Jenny" made her memorable triumph at Covent Garden it was the Queen's bouquet which was the first to be cast at the feet of the singer. In those bright, happy days Victoria stood in the forefront of the national life. She patronised all that was best in literature, art, and the drama, and gave her sympathy and help to the philanthropies of the time. Theatres which aimed at royal patronage were obliged to conform to the Queen's taste, and gradually the coarse survivals of a ruder time were swept from the stage. Society took its cue from her, and the Court became as pure as a good woman could make it.

The Queen undoubtedly loved the gaieties of town in the early years of her reign; but as the little ones began to cluster about her knees, she longed for the quietude of country life, drawn to it also by her thoughtful, studious husband. We find her running away in the height of the season to enjoy a quiet time with her husband and children amidst the flowery glades of Claremont. On one of these occasions "Vicky" and "Bertie" came to the Queen's room to wish her many happy returns of her birthday, dressed Tyrolese fashion, and looking such sweet little foreigners that their mother hardly knew them. This little surprise was planned by the Prince and the Duchess of Kent, and affords a pleasing glimpse into the home life of the royal pair.

Her Majesty was no stickler for extreme Court etiquette when it caused actual discomfort to others. It had been the custom for the sovereign to hold drawing-rooms seated upon the throne, thus obliging those presented to mount the steps to kiss hands, and then retire backwards — no easy task with a voluminous train behind. To lessen the difficulties of the ladies, the Queen received them at the foot of the throne, and permitted them, after retiring a few steps backwards, to take their trains over their arms and resume their natural walk.

The same consideration was shown by the Queen to her maids of honour; no weary standing on tired feet, no hours of reading aloud, of which poor Miss Burney complained in the days of old Queen Charlotte, and certainly the ladies did not get their ears boxed for misdemeanour, a not uncommon thing in the "good old times." Her Majesty treated her ladies as friends; they sang and played with her, accompanied her upon horseback or in the carriage, and appear to have had few actual duties beyond these, and handing the Queen her bouquet at dinner. She addressed them by their Christian names, and when they returned to residence received them with a kiss and inquiries regarding the home circle which they had just left. One thing the Queen did rigidly exact, and that was punctuality.

Those who have been about Her Majesty invariably speak of the charm of her conversation and presence. Lady Bloomfield, writing of a musical evening at Windsor, says: "I enjoy nothing so much as seeing the Queen in that nice quiet way, and I often wish that those who don't know Her Majesty could see how kind and generous she is when she is perfectly at her ease and able to throw off the restraint and form which must and ought to be observed when she is in public." The Baroness Bunsen writes to her son in the same strain after lunching with the Queen at Stafford House: "The Queen looked well and charming, and I could not help the same reflection that I have often made before, that she is the only piece of female royalty I ever saw who was also a creature such as God Almighty has created. Her smile is a real smile, her grace is natural, although it has received a high polish from cultivation — there is nothing artificial about her." In evidence of the delight which this lady felt in dining with the Queen, she relates that in spite of a severe cold, which inconvenienced her to the extent of necessitating the use of six handkerchiefs during the morning, she availed herself of the privilege of dining with the Queen in the evening. We fancy in former reigns a bad cold would have been welcomed as a convenient excuse for not obeying the royal command. Fortunately for the Baroness, it was the time when ladies carried their mouchoirs in dainty little bags, so she was not limited in her supply.

Lady Lyttelton, the second daughter of Earl Spencer, who had been lady-in-waiting since the Queen's accession, had, as we have seen, been entrusted by Her Majesty with the charge of the royal children. She was a kind, motherly lady, admirably fitted for this important office, which she held for eight years. The royal mother, however, remained herself the chief authority in nursery matters, and supervised every detail of the children's training. In drawing up some rules for their education, she said: "The greatest maxim of all is — that the children should be brought up as simply as possible, and in as domestic a way as possible; that, not interfering with their lessons, they should be as much as possible with their parents, and learn to place their greatest confidence in them in all things.... Religious training is best given to a child at its mother's knee." Apropos of the latter, there is a story of that brilliantly clever child, the Princess Royal. The Queen was reading the Bible with her little daughter, and came to the passage, "God created man in His own image, in the image of God created He him," upon which "Vicky," who had a sense of beauty and fitness, exclaimed, "But, mamma, surely not Dr. Pratorious?" This gentleman was secretary to Prince Albert, and by no means good-looking.

When the children were young, all goods purchased for their wear were submitted to the Queen, and it was at her command that only the plainest fare was sent to the nursery, "quite poor living — only a bit of roast meat and perhaps a plain pudding," one of the servants told Baron Bunsen, adding that the Queen would have made "an admirable poor man's wife." As the Princesses grew older, they were taught to take care of their clothes, even to that old-maidish custom of rolling up the bonnet-strings. One of the chief anxieties of the royal mother was that her children should be kept free from the enervating influences of rank and power, self-indulgence and flattery. They were taught consideration for the feelings of others, and to be universally polite. The Prince of Wales was a perfect little gentleman, and when his mother said, "Make your bow, sir," upon introducing him to a visitor, he did it with charming grace. We find the Queen constantly speaking of him as "good little Bertie." The Princess Royal was the delight of the Court and of the people; but her mother had to exercise severe discipline to keep her in order. For example, when Dr. Brown, of Windsor, entered the service of Prince Albert, the little princesses, hearing their father address him as "Brown," used the same form of speech. The Queen corrected them, and told them to say "Dr. Brown." All obeyed except "Vicky," who was threatened with "bed" if she transgressed again. Next morning, when the Doctor presented himself to the royal family, the young Princess, looking straight at him, said, "Good morning, Brown!" Then, seeing the eyes of her mother fixed upon her, she rose and, with a curtsey, continued, "and good night, Brown, for I am going to bed," and she walked resolutely away to her punishment. This was the same young lady who, at three years old, motioned away her governess, Lady Lyttelton, with, "N'approchez pas moi, moi ne veut pas vous."

When quite young, the children were taken by their royal parents to see a review of the Guards in honour of the Prince of Wales's birthday. The troops marched past the royal family, presenting arms, and afterwards fired a feu de joie. This rather frightened the Princess Royal, and when the band struck up "God Save the Queen," fearing that there was going to be another volley, she put her hands to her ears, and shocked her mother dreadfully. The repartee of the little Princess would have been "delicious" if some one had whispered in her ear that her own mamma had done the same thing when the cannon thundered on her coronation day.

Thus early the royal children were made accustomed to pageants, and we find that on the occasion just referred to the Prince of Wales and tiny Princess Alice stood throughout the manoeuvres almost motionless, which led one of the ladies to exclaim that she had never seen such good children.

Another story shows that the Princess Royal had a sense of dignity regarding her small performances. A certain Major Douglas had sent her a handsome present of toys, and when he next had an audience, Her Majesty desired the little Princess to thank him for them, which she did very nicely. When Lady Lyttelton took her down to the Queen's room, she mentioned in an undertone that the child had delivered her speech very well, at which the Queen turned round to her, and said: "Well, Pussy, and what did you say?" The consequential little mite answered, "I said — I said my speech."

A notable figure in the Queen's married life was that trusted friend and adviser, Baron Stockmar, who for seventeen years moved quietly in the background of the Court. He was an army physician who became attached to the suite of Prince Leopold, the Queen's uncle, and was with him at Claremont when his young wife, the Princess Charlotte, died. Later on he accompanied Prince Leopold when he became King of Belgium. Upon the Queen's accession, Uncle Leopold despatched the trusted Stockmar to England to watch over the welfare of his niece. It was not, however, until after the Queen's marriage that he became a permanent figure in her household. What "the Duke" was to the nation, "the Baron" became to the Court, and the wags dubbed him the "Old Original." He was a man of sterling qualities; upright, sagacious, with a vast amount of knowledge of the world, and was equally useful beside a sick-bed or at a writing-table. In the royal nursery he was a perfect oracle, and is reported to have said, "The nursery gives me more trouble than the government of a kingdom would do." Under his judicious management the delicate little Princess Royal became so fat and well that he was able to write of her, "She is as round as a barrel," and the Queen said in one of her letters, "Pussy's cheeks are on the point of bursting." The queer old German Baron was a kind of fairy godfather to the little folks; it was to his room they ran with their latest toy, or when they wanted a story. The Princess Royal, however, was his favourite, her smart wit delighting him vastly.

The Baron was, as might be expected, a privileged person. He was permitted to sit at Her Majesty's dinner table in trousers, while other old gentlemen shivered in "shorts." Immediately the meal was over he would be seen walking off to his own room without ceremony. He never sacrificed his comfort to etiquette. When the spring came, he suddenly disappeared, without any adieux; then would follow letters of regret from his royal master and mistress, and, after spending a few months with his wife and family in his native Coburg, the Baron would return to Windsor as mysteriously as he had disappeared, and resume his role of chief adviser and general referee.

The Queen had now what she called "a home of her own," in contradistinction to the royal palaces, having purchased the beautiful estate of Osborne, in the Isle of Wight, and built herself there a marine residence at a cost of £200,000. The grounds were artistically laid out under the direction of that most skilled of landscape gardeners, Prince Albert. The original estate was added to, until now, as a coachman in the island will tell you, the Queen can drive for twelve miles without going outside her own domain. The house-warming at Osborne took place in September, 1846, when a maid of honour threw an old slipper for good luck as the Queen entered her new abode, and at the Prince's suggestion an appropriate German hymn was sung, beginning:

"God bless our going out, nor less
Our coming in."

Later on, to celebrate one of the Queen's birthdays, the Swiss Cottage was erected in the grounds for the use of the children. There the boys learned carpentering, under their father's direction, and the princesses studied culinary arts in a model kitchen and dairy, entertained their parents to repasts prepared with their own hands, and made dishes for the poor. The Cottage also contained a museum of natural history, the contents being largely collected by the royal children. In front were the gardens, one for each child, which they tended themselves, under the direction of a gardener, who instructed them not only in flower culture, but in the rearing of fruit and vegetables. Few children have, indeed, been taught more thoroughly how to use their hands than the Queen's family. Her Majesty and the Prince were charmed with their beautiful retreat, with the woods sloping down to the blue sea, and in summer evenings they walked in the plantation to listen to the nightingales, which grew so familiar with the Prince that they would answer his whistle. The entire building and laying out of the Osborne estate was not completed until 1851, the portion known as the Pavilion being occupied meantime.

The year 1845 was famous for another of the Queen's Bals Masque. The period chosen was between 1740 and 1750, and the prevailing feature of powdered wigs gave it the name of the Powder Ball. The time was not one at which the dress was very becoming, and when the royal fiat went forth ladies were horrified at the idea of wearing powdered toupees, pomatumed curls, and wide-spreading hoops. The costume was arranged, however, to look as becoming as possible, and the ladies became reconciled to it when they discovered that powdered hair made the complexion look more brilliant, and that if the hoop disguised the figure the stomacher displayed it. Half the great houses in London were turned into milliners' shops, and filled with stuffs, patterns, and drawings of costumes. Society dames studied the family portraits of the period, and the grandmothers' heirlooms were in great requisition, The Queen, dressed as the Lady of the Feast, wore a magnificent brocade covered with point lace drawn from the hoards of her grandmother, Queen Charlotte; while Prince Albert looked bravely in a scarlet velvet coat and gold waistcoat. They opened the ball with a polonaise, and closed it with Sir Roger de Coverley. It would take a long list to mention the celebrities and beauties who graced the occasion. The Duke of Wellington was there in a marshal's uniform of the period, which hung so loosely about his spare limbs as to render him almost unrecognisable. It was said that no one would have known him but for his nose. He walked about with his lovely daughter-in-law, the Marchioness of Douro, who wore a brocade trimmed with lace flounces which had once belonged to the vestment of a pope. Miss Burdett-Coutts, the banker's heiress, was then just coming into society, and the jewels she wore at the ball were the talk of the town for many weeks afterwards, prominent amongst them being a necklace which had belonged to Marie Antoinette.

In 1848 the Prince leased Balmoral Castle as a hunting-box, and the royal pair had then their Island and Highland homes (the present Castle was not built until some years later). Old Balmoral was a pretty little grey castle in the Old Scottish style, situated amongst the picturesque mountain scenery of the valley of the Dee. It was originally a farmhouse, and had gradually grown into palatial appearance, although at the time when the Queen first lived there it was little larger than an ordinary gentleman's house. It was surrounded by primitive huts, with the peat smoke issuing from holes in the roofs — a solitary, picturesque, and peaceful spot, with the deer creeping stealthily round the house. Here, 'mid Dee's "rushing tide" and the heather-clad hills, the Queen enjoyed each autumn the free, outdoor life which was a passion with her. She climbed the mountains on her Highland pony, explored the solitudes, took refuge from storms in shepherds' huts, was carried over marshy ground on a plaid slung between two Highlanders, had "scratch" meals in wayside inns, and accompanied her husband on his deer-stalking expeditions, remaining out sometimes for nine hours at a time. She was fond of sketching amongst the hills, and one day had an amusing encounter with a herd laddie, who found that his flock were timid at the sight of her upon the sheep track.

"Gang out of the road, lady, and let the sheep gang by," he cried. Finding that his appeal produced no effect, he shouted yet louder, "I say, gang back, will you, and let the sheep pass!"

"Do you know, boy, whom you are speaking to?" asked the Queen's attendant.

"I dinna know, and I dinna care," replied the exasperated lad; "that's the sheep's road, and she has no business to stand there."

"But it is the Queen," was the reply.

"Well," replied the astonished boy, "why don't she put on clothes so that folks would know her?"

A Minister of State was always in attendance when the Queen was at Balmoral, and we fear that some of those stately gentlemen rubbed their eyes and could not believe their senses when they beheld the Monarch of the British Empire and her illustrious Consort living like small gentlefolk, in a small house, with small rooms, and having only a few attendants. The Clerk of the Council, who accompanied Lord John Russell, the Prime Minister, to Balmoral, exclaimed in horror, "There are no soldiers, and the whole guard of the sovereign and the royal family is a single policeman," adding further that the Queen was to be seen running in and out of the house all day long, and visiting the old women in the cottages unattended. Worse still, Lord Palmerston found the Queen sallying forth for a walk in the midst of heavy rain with a great hood over her bonnet, concealing all the features except her eyes; and poor Lord John Russell, after dining for the first time at Balmoral, actually saw the dining-room cleared for the Queen and Prince to take lessons in reels and strathspeys from a Highland dancing-master, to the tune of a fiddle. The royal children, too, clad in kilts and tartans, wandered by the hillside, paddled in the burn, played with the cottage children, and on Sundays accompanied their parents to the little Presbyterian church of Crathie on the other side the Dee. One wonders that society did not refuse to attend the next Drawing-Room, and that the Bench of Bishops did not travel express to Balmoral! Never has the Queen shown herself greater than when she has put aside the trappings of royalty and stood forth in the grandeur on her own womanhood. Victoria of England is great enough to be herself.

It would seem, indeed, that the Queen was safer at Balmoral, guarded by one policeman, than in London, for in May, 1849, Her Majesty was again fired at when driving along Constitution Hill, this time by a mad Irishman, William Hamilton, and one can sympathise with the indignant words of Lord Shaftesbury (then Lord Ashley) when he said, "While the profligate George IV. passed through a life of selfishness and sin without a single proved attempt to take it, this mild and virtuous young woman has four times already been exposed to imminent peril." But the good man thanked God that the Queen and her husband were what they were, with a moral Court, domestic virtues, and some public activity in philanthropic things. Nothing daunted by this attack, in the August following the Queen paid her first visit to Ireland, accompanied by the Prince and four of the children. She landed at the Cove of Cork, which henceforth became Queenstown. All sorts of dreadful things had been prophesied, but nothing could exceed the loyalty and enthusiasm shown by the people. From one of the triumphal arches a live dove, sweet emblem of peace, fluttered into the

Queen's lap, and a stout old lady in Dublin exclaimed, "O Queen dear! make one of them dear children Prince Patrick, and all Ireland will die for you." The hint was not forgotten; when on the 1st of May, 1850, the Queen's seventh child was born, he received the name of Arthur Patrick Albert.

It is noticeable that at this period of the Queen's life she began to take active interest in social questions and in the condition of the working people. We find that she and the Prince sent for Lord Ashley, and asked his advice as to what they could do to ameliorate the condition of the working classes, and they entered most sympathetically into his schemes for the better housing of the poor, and his humane legislation on behalf of the women and children employed in mines. The keen anxiety felt by the Queen to promote peaceful industry and the brotherhood of man, the world over, had an outcome in that memorable Peace Festival, when all nationalities displayed their products and industries — the Great Exhibition of 1851. We are used to exhibitions now, but this one was counted a marvel, and even to-day old people refer to it as an epoch in their lives. "It was when I was in London in '51, you know, my dear," they will say. The Exhibition was opened by Her Majesty at nine o'clock on the morning of the 1st of May, 1851. There were thirty-four thousand people in the building, and nearly a million on the line of route; but instead of the riots and disturbances prophesied as the result of this vast gathering of all nationalities, the Queen was rejoiced to hear that, like her coronation, it was a white day — not one accident or police case. One who was present at the opening has told the writer that never had the Queen looked so radiantly happy as she did when she entered the beautiful Palace of Crystal, leaning on the arm of her handsome husband, to whose untiring efforts this great and unique enterprise was due. She wore a pink silk poplin, of Irish manufacture, trimmed with white lace, and upon her head a tiara of diamonds, with white ostrich feathers drooping gracefully on either side. The Prince of Wales, then a little fellow of nine, held her hand, while the Princess Royal, dressed in white with a wreath of roses, held that of her father, and the people said how like she was to her mother when she was young. It was, indeed, a complete and beautiful triumph, and the Queen speaks of it as being the proudest and happiest day of her life.

THE LATER MARRIED LIFE OF QUEEN VICTORIA

THE Exhibition year of 1851, which marked an epoch in the history of the nation, marked also the meridian of Queen Victoria's married life. There seemed to be scarcely a cloud upon her horizon. She rejoiced in the beautiful children who clustered at her knee, and in the husband who, after eleven years of wedded life, was more than ever her beau ideal of all that was noble, good, and true; and it was her further happiness to find that the country was beginning to appreciate him too. The overwhelming success of the Great Exhibition, Prince Albert's own creation, silenced for the present his detractors, and Ministers were now eager to tell the Queen that it was a wonderful conception, and that the Prince was a very remarkable man, to which Her Majesty was apt to reply in effect, if not in words, "Didn't I tell you so?" Shortly after her engagement she had told Lord Melbourne that the Prince was perfection, and the old man smiled at a girl-bride's enthusiasm; but the day came when he wrote to the Queen: "You said when you were going to be married that he [the Prince] was perfection, which I thought a little exaggerated then; but really I think now that it is in some degree realised."

Such happiness and content was naturally reflected in the Queen's appearance at this period. Her face, which in her girlhood was bright and pretty, had taken a more enduring charm in its softened, thoughtful expression, and those who were about her speak of the spiritual serenity of her countenance and the lovableness of her disposition. Baron Stockmar, who had watched her long and critically, said: "The Queen improves greatly. She makes daily advances in discernment and experience; the candour, the love of truth, the fairness, the considerateness with which she judges men and things are truly delightful, and the ingenuous self-knowledge with which she speaks about herself is simply charming." For fourteen years she had wielded the greatest sceptre in the world, and the experience thus gained was showing itself in her mastery of the duties and responsibilities of her position. The young Queen who had resented the downfall of the Melbourne Ministry because it removed loved friends from her side had learned to regard such changes from the constitutional standpoint, and not from private feeling. Landseer, who had many opportunities of judging, told Caroline Fox that he thought the Queen's intellect superior to any woman's in Europe. Her memory was so remarkable that he had heard her recall "the exact words of speeches made years before, which the speakers had themselves forgotten." The Queen had now developed into a sagacious stateswoman with whom Cabinet Ministers had to reckon.

Her Court was at once the purest and one of the most splendid in Europe, and the season which followed the opening of the Great Exhibition was the most brilliant of any since the Queen's accession; the town literally swarmed with distinguished people from all parts of the world. The two chief society events were the Queen's Stuart Ball and the City of London Ball. The strong dramatic element in the Queen's character led her to adopt the masque as her favourite form of entertainment. Fancy balls illustrating the Plantagenet and Georgian periods had already been given, and on the 13th of June, 1851, the famous Stuart Ball, to illustrate the time of the Merry Monarch, took place at Buckingham Palace. The Queen and Prince Albert appeared in superb dresses of the period, and Her Majesty's pretty fair hair was plaited with pearls beneath a crown of diamonds. It might be described as a "gentlemen's night," for they took the palm for smart dresses; gay cavaliers were they all, with love-locks, collars and cuffs of Honiton lace, and such a profusion of ribbons as had never been seen before. They wore them hanging in bunches like a Highlander's philibeg, and even their shirt sleeves were bound and ornamented with ribbons. Of course "the Duke" was there, but he drew the line at love-locks, and wore his own scanty grey hair, which made him a marked figure in the crowd with flowing curls. It is interesting to note that Mr. Gladstone figured as Sir Leoline Jenkins, Judge in the High Court of Admiralty, and wore "a black velvet coat turned up with blue satin, ruffles and collar of old point lace, black breeches and stockings, and shoes with spreading bows."

About a month later came the ball at the Guildhall given by the Mayor and Corporation to the Queen in celebration of the Great Exhibition. Her Majesty drove from Buckingham Palace through dense crowds of people, literally shouting in every tongue, and to see her return more than a million people waited in the streets until three o'clock in the morning. The ball itself was the most amusing affair possible, many of the guests not having the least idea of Court, or even of ordinary good behaviour. A nobleman who was present relates that the ladies passed the Queen at a run, and then returned to stare at her. Some of the gentlemen passed with their arms round the ladies' waists, and others holding them by the hand at arm's length, as if going to dance a minuet. But when one man kissed his hand to the Queen, her risibility could stand no more, and she went off into one of those uncontrollable fits of laughter for which Her Majesty is rather famous, and doubtless the Lord Mayor's guests thought this the best part of the entertainment.

In accordance with the spirit of peace and goodwill to all men with which the Queen and Prince Albert had initiated the Exhibition, religious, philanthropic, and scientific institutions received a marked share of attention. A monster meeting on behalf of the Society for the Propagation of the Gospel in Foreign Parts was held, at which Prince Albert presided, and made a remarkably fine speech; and he was also active on behalf of the British Association. At length there came a lull in the routs, meetings, and festivities — town was out of town, for the Queen had left for the Highlands.

It was on this occasion that Her Majesty first travelled by the Great Northern Railway. She halted at Peterborough to receive her "kind, good master," Bishop Davys. Canon Davys, the son of the Bishop, has told the present writer that Her Majesty never visited his father at Peterborough Palace, as some writers allege, knowing the simple life which he led; but she never failed to invite him to meet her at the station when she passed through Peterborough on her way to Scotland. She always received her old tutor in the royal saloon carriage like a valued friend, and would show him her children, and talk over their futures with him. Canon Davys attended as chaplain on such occasions, and he well remembers the Queen bringing forward Prince Alfred (the present Duke of Saxe-Coburg), and saying, "We are going to make this boy a sailor." Proceeding to Edinburgh, the Queen passed a night at Holyrood Palace. It may not be generally known that Her Majesty has always shown a sympathetic interest in the fate of Mary Queen of Scots, and this her first sojourn in the Palace so intimately connected with her was full of romantic interest, and she told Sir Archibald Alison that she was glad that she was descended from Mary Stuart and not from Elizabeth Tudor. From Holyrood the royal party proceeded to Balmoral, which had now been purchased by Prince Albert, he having previously rented it. Here the autumn was passed by the Queen in that free, simple manner which she loved — walking, driving, riding, sketching, and visiting the cottagers. At first the simple Scotch folk were a little disconcerted by the royal visits; but when one of the old women expressed her nervousness to the Queen, Her Majesty replied that she hoped that they would not allow any feeling of that kind to trouble them as she was just a woman like themselves. The following story will illustrate the feeling which speedily grew up between the Queen and her poorer neighbours. A man from Balmoral was being examined as a witness before the jury, when the presiding judge spoke rather sharply to him. "Just allow me to tak' time, my lord," said the man; "I'm no accustomed to sic a company"; adding to the bystanders, after he left the witness-box, "The Queen has been to my hut, and she speaks pleasantly and draws pretty pictures for the bairns. I would far rather speak to the Queen than to yon chap in the big wig."

After leaving the Highlands the Queen paid her first visit to Liverpool and Manchester. The festivities at Liverpool were marred by a steady downpour; but at Manchester the weather was more propitious, and an interesting demonstration took place in Peel Park, where eighty thousand school children, belonging to the various religious denominations, were assembled. The "canny" Manchester folk had hit on the right thing to please the Queen's motherly heart. Her look of delight as she gazed at the children, ranged tier above tier, fourteen deep, was long remembered by the people. Continuing her journey to London, the Queen paid a farewell visit to the Exhibition, where she found Mary Kerlynack, the plucky old woman who walked all the way from her native Cornwall to see the wonder, still hovering about the doors, and appeared ready to cry when the Queen looked at her. The Exhibition was closed on the 15th of October, the twelfth anniversary of Her Majesty's betrothal to Prince Albert. Its success had exceeded the most sanguine expectations; yet a feeling of sadness seemed to be in the heart of the Queen and of the nation, a half-conscious foreboding that this Peace Festival was to be the herald of a darker instead of a brighter time, for already the war-clouds were gathering which burst in the Crimean war.

While the Queen was staying at Balmoral in the autumn of 1852 she received a pleasant surprise in the shape of a legacy of £250,000, left to her by Mr. John Camden Neale, a man of penurious habits, who had accumulated this large sum by denying himself the necessaries of life. When one of Mr. Neale's executors came to Balmoral to make the communication, the Queen laughingly said that she "could not think what had led the old gentleman to do it," and at first she refused to accept the legacy. Finding subsequently that there were no relations to inherit, she decided to take the money, first increasing Mr. Neale's bequest to his executors of £100 to £1,000. She also provided for his old housekeeper, for whom he had made no provision, although she had been with him for twenty-six years. It was while still in Scotland that the Queen received the news of the death of the Duke of Wellington, which filled her with grief. "One cannot think of the country without the Duke, our immortal hero," she said. A curious coincidence occurred on the morning when the Queen received the tidings. She was out walking, and suddenly missed the watch given her by the Duke, which she always wore. Later in the morning a servant returned to the Queen, who was sketching at the Glassalt Shiel, to say that the watch was all right at the Castle, but at the same time handing Lord Derby's telegram giving the news of the Duke's death. Her Majesty returned to town to witness the funeral procession, which was the most remarkable death pageant of her reign. It took place on the 18th of November, 1852, and passed to St. Paul's through streets draped in black; a "masquerade in ink," Dickens rather flippantly called it. Duty to the Crown had always been the mainspring of Wellington's life, and his devotion to the Queen, over whom he had watched with a fatherly pride from her earliest years, was quite romantic.

On the 7th of April, 1853, the Queen's eighth child and fourth son was born at Buckingham Palace, and received, among others, the name of Leopold, after her beloved uncle, the King of the Belgians. Only three weeks before this event an alarming fire had broken out at Windsor Castle close to the white drawing-room, where the Queen and Prince were sitting; but Her Majesty displayed her usual intrepidity, and received no harm. A few months after her confinement, she had her family "down with the measles," and suffered a slight attack herself. Happily all quickly recovered, and in the succeeding August the royal party visited Ireland to open the Exhibition of Art and Industry at Dublin.

In the autumn of 1853 the Queen was considerably "worried" by a revival of the charges of "foreign influence" directed against her husband. War was now imminent with Russia, and the popular feeling was in its favour; still, there was hesitation and dissension in the Cabinet, and this was attributed to the influence "behind the throne." The feeling displayed drew from the Queen a letter to Lord Aberdeen, in which she said that the Prince was one and the same with herself, and that attacks upon him were the same as attacks upon the throne. When Parliament met in January, 1854, the calumnies against the Prince were refuted in both Houses, and for the first time the right of the Prince to advise the sovereign — his wife — was officially accepted. Shortly after this dark cloud had been lifted, the Queen kept the fourteenth anniversary of her marriage at Windsor, when the royal children performed a Masque of the Seasons, which the Baroness Bunsen, who was present, describes as being a wonderfully pretty sight. Spring was represented by Princess Alice, Summer by the Princess Royal, Autumn by Prince Alfred, and Winter by the Prince of Wales. A separate tableau was given for each season, and the children recited suitable verses from Thomson's "Seasons." As a finale, all the seasons stood in a group while the little Princess Helena, dressed as Britannia, pronounced a blessing on their parents. The Queen's elder children were now entering upon their teens, and it was a conscientious duty with her that they should be rightly trained for their high position. When some years previously Mr. Birch had been appointed tutor to the Prince of Wales, the Queen wrote: "It is an important step, and God's blessing be upon it; for upon the good education of princes, and especially those who are destined to govern, the welfare of the world, in these days, very greatly depends." The instruction which she had given for the religious training of the Princess Royal was followed in the case of all the royal children. "I am quite clear," wrote the Queen in a memorandum, that "she should have great reverence for God and religion, but that she should have the feeling of devotion and love which our heavenly Father encourages His earthly children to have for Him, and not one of fear and trembling; and that the thoughts of death and an after life should not be represented in an alarming and forbidding view, and that she should be made to know as yet no difference of creeds, and not think that she can only pray on her knees, or that those who do not kneel are less fervent and devout in their prayers." Her Majesty, indeed, kept the religious instruction of her children largely in her own hands. A story is told that when the Archdeacon of London was catechising the young Princes he said, "Your governess deserves great credit for instructing you so thoroughly." At which the boys piped up, "Oh, but it is mamma who teaches us our Catechism." It is not perhaps generally known that the Queen occasionally taught a Bible-class for the children of those in attendance at Buckingham Palace, and that, it having come to her knowledge that the children of the servants and attendants at the Palace were without the means for ordinary instruction, she commanded that a school should be started for them in Palace Street, Pimlico, and herself showed the greatest interest in its management.

Her Majesty encouraged her own boys to choose their profession when they were quite young, and had them educated in accordance with their choice, excepting of course the Prince of Wales, who was born to wear the purple, and had no option in the matter. His training and education were, however, a conscientious study with his parents, who placed him successively under the care of Mr. Birch and Mr. Gibbs, and when in 1859 he entered Cambridge University, General the Hon. Robert Bruce, brother of Lord Elgin, accompanied him as "Governor." The attachment of "Princey," as the heir to the throne was frequently called by the Queen's ladies, to his tutors was quite touching. Lady Canning writes from Windsor Castle in June, 1852: "Mr. Birch [the tutor] left yesterday. It has been a terrible sorrow to the Prince of Wales, who has done no end of touching things since he heard that he was to lose him, three weeks ago. He is such an affectionate, dear little boy; his little notes and presents, which Mr. Birch used to find on his pillow, were really too moving."

Prince Alfred early expressed his wish to be a sailor, and he was sent from home at twelve years of age to pursue his studies in a separate establishment, at the Royal Lodge, Windsor Park, under the care of Lieutenant Cowell, a young officer of engineers, afterwards Sir John Cowell, K.C.B., Master of Her Majesty's Household; later on, the sailor-Prince had an establishment at Alverbank, near Portsmouth, for the greater convenience of his naval studies. Prince Arthur decided to be a soldier, and began his training when nine years of age, under Captain Elphinstone, of the Engineers, afterwards Sir Howard Elphinstone. Thus the education of the three elder Princes was settled.

Great grief was felt by the Queen and Prince Albert when, in 1851, Lady Lyttelton retired from the post of governess to the royal children. She was succeeded by Lady Caroline Barrington, sister of Earl Grey, who held the important position for twenty-four years, and was greatly beloved by the young Princesses. The Princess Royal became very remarkable as a girl as she had been clever as a child, and the constant companionship of her scholarly father developed her natural intellect to an astonishing degree. She was more of a woman at fifteen than most girls are at twenty. Princess Alice inherited her mother's affectionate nature and musical voice, and we find on festive occasions in the royal household that "Alice" did the recitations and speechifying.

A girl of such strong personality as the Princess Royal needed the curb occasionally, and how promptly the royal mother applied it is illustrated by the following story. When about thirteen years old the Princess accompanied her mother to a military review, and seemed disposed, as she sat in the carriage, to be a little coquettish with some of the young officers of the escort. The Queen gave her some warning looks without avail, and presently the young Princess dangled her handkerchief over the side of the carriage and dropped it — evidently for the purpose. There was an immediate rush of young officers to pick it up; but the royal mother bid the gentlemen desist from their gallant intention, and turning to poor unfortunate "Vicky," said in a stern voice, "Now, my daughter, pick up your handkerchief yourself." There was no help for it; the footman let down the steps, and the young Princess did her mother's bidding, with flaming cheeks and a saucy toss of the head, though. Another time it was "Princey" who received a wholesome lesson. He was riding in company with his father, and for once forgot his usual politeness, and neglected to acknowledge the salute of a passer-by. Prince Albert observing it said, "Now, my son, go back and return that man's bow," which he accordingly did. One might go on multiplying these stories, but sufficient has been said to show that the Queen's children were taught respectful obedience to their parents and elders in a manner not common to-day.

It always seems to have been the fate of English queens to have one important war. Queen Elizabeth fought the Spaniard and vanquished the Armada, Mary had her disastrous war with the French and lost Calais, Queen Anne's reign was famous for the victories of Marlborough, and Victoria had the Crimean war. It was on the 28th of February, 1854, that Her Majesty signed a formal declaration of war with Russia. In doing so she acted from the strongest sense of duty. The nation had made up its mind that Russian aggressions in the East must be checked, and the war-cry in the country was too strong to be disregarded. It is quite evident that the Queen and Prince Consort would have avoided the contest if they could have found an honourable means of doing so. In reply to the King of Prussia, who wrote at the eleventh hour urging peace, the Queen sent a letter full of patriotic spirit, and ending with the famous quotation:

"Beware of entrance to a quarrel; but being in,
Bear it, that the opposer may beware of thee."

For the next two years her life was passed in consuming anxiety regarding this campaign. First she bid God-speed to her gallant troops as they started for the seat of war; then came the farewell to the magnificent war fleet as it sailed for the Baltic under command of Sir Charles Napier, and the launching and christening of the Royal Albert, a monster ironclad sent to the Crimea with reinforcements after the battle of Inkermann. With throbbing heart the Queen received the tidings of the battles of Alva, Inkermann, Balaclava, and the Charge of the Light Brigade; and as the cry of the widow and orphan began to be heard in the land, she and the Prince felt that something must be done to aid the distressed. In October, 1854, the Patriotic Fund, headed by Prince Consort, was started. Subscriptions poured in from every part of the empire, and all over England concerts, theatricals, and entertainments were held to aid the good work. By March, 1855, the Fund had reached the sum of one million. The royal children drew and painted pictures, which were exhibited at Burlington House, and sold in aid of the Fund. The "Battle Field," painted by the clever Princess Royal, brought 250 guineas; "Bertie's" production realised only 55 guineas — rather trying for a boy to be so far behind his sister — while the drawings of the younger children brought 30 guineas apiece. The Queen and her ladies spent much of their time in knitting and sewing garments for the soldiers and preparing bandages, while "Vicky" and "Alice," with all the enthusiasm of young girls, longed and even planned to go out and join Florence Nightingale and her noble band of nurses at Scutari. In fact, the sympathy and enthusiasm of the royal children were stirred to the highest pitch, and we find one of the young Princes saying to Lord Cardigan, when he returned to Windsor to visit Her Majesty, "Do hurry back and take Sebastopol, or else it will kill mamma."

Frequent letters were written by the Queen to the seat of war, expressing concern at the gross mismanagement of the commissariat in the early part of the campaign, and vehemently urging that every effort should be made to save the brave men from privation. During a war debate in Parliament in January, 1855, Mr. Augustus Stafford thrilled his hearers by telling them that he had seen a wounded man in the hospital, after hearing one of the Queen's sympathetic letters read, propose her health in a glass of bark and quinine. "It is a bitter cup for a loyal toast," said Mr. Stafford, to which the man replied, "Yes; and but for the words of the Queen I could not have got it down." In opening Parliament during this period of national sorrow, for the first time the Queen's silvery accents failed her, and the speech from the throne was read by her in broken accents and with tears streaming down her face. "It was a sight never to be forgotten," says one who was present, "for the whole assembly was convulsed with grief; there was scarcely one present who had not the loss of a dear one to mourn." When the melancholy contingents of wounded began to return home, the Queen constantly visited the sufferers in the military hospitals; and it having occurred to her that the men would value a token of regard from her own hands, a most pathetic and interesting ceremony took place on the 18th of May, 1855, at the Horse Guards, when she presented war medals to the officers and men disabled or home on sick leave. Sad-eyed indeed was the Queen as they filed past her with gaunt forms, pallid faces, and maimed and disabled bodies; but it was beautiful to see how the faces of the men brightened as she spoke kind and grateful words to them. An amusing story is told by the Earl of Malmesbury of the "density" of the Minister for War, Lord Panmure, on this occasion. "Was the Queen touched?" asked a lady of him, referring to the pathetic spectacle. "Bless my soul, no!" was the reply; "she had a brass railing before her, and no one could touch her." "Was she moved, I mean?" persisted the lady. "Moved!" answered Lord Panmure; "she had no occasion to move." The sequel to this lack of intelligence on the part of the Minister of War may be found in the fact that the Queen's quick eyes had detected many flaws in the management of the military hospitals during her visits, and she had addressed remonstrances to Lord Panmure on the subject. It was owing to the Queen's efforts that, after the war, the beautiful military hospital at Netley was built.

In connection with the distribution of the Crimean war medals, a story is told of an old lady who kept the Swiss Cottage on the Duke of Bedford's estate at Endsleigh. When Her Majesty was paying a visit to the Cottage, the old lady thought, "Now's my chance," and plucking up heart she said, "Please, your Majesty, ma'am, I had a son, a faithful subject of your

Majesty, and he was killed in your wars out in the Crimea, and I wants his medal." "And you shall have it," replied the Queen, with a soft voice and melting eye, as she took the old woman's hand.

The friendly alliance entered into between France and England during the Crimean war was the occasion of an interchange of visits between the sovereigns. The Emperor Napoleon, with his lovely young Empress Eugenie, visited Windsor in April, 1855, and a few months later the Queen and Prince Albert returned the visit, taking the Prince of Wales and the Princess Royal along with them. A series of brilliant entertainments took place in Paris, and the friendship between the Queen and the amiable and lovely Eugenie, which has lasted until the present time, was begun. Often one fancies that the two royal widows must sadly talk together of those bright, happy times. The two children enjoyed their visit to Paris immensely, and the Prince of Wales conceived the brilliant idea that he and his sister might remain behind and continue the festivities after the departure of their parents. The Empress made the usual reply which hostesses give to importunate juveniles — that their "papa and mamma would not be able to spare them," to which "Bertie" replied, "Oh, they can do without us; there are six more at home."

Shortly after the return of the Queen from France, the joy bells rang through the land that at length Sebastopol had fallen, and the war was practically at an end.

The years 1856-57 were spent largely by the Queen amongst the returning warriors. It was a season of military reviews and decorations, and the enthusiasm of the troops at Aldershot, as Her Majesty rode down the lines on her chestnut charger in the uniform of a field marshal, draped below the waist with a dark blue skirt, was unbounded; and when on another occasion she delivered a stirring speech to the soldiers from her carriage, the scene of excitement beggars description — "bearskins and shakos were thrown into the air, dragoons waved their sabres, and shouts rang all down the lines." The Queen showed her appreciation of Miss Nightingale's noble work by inviting her to Balmoral immediately after she had settled in the newly built castle. On the 26th of June, 1857, came the crowning act of the Queen in the Crimean period, when she distributed the Victoria Crosses, a badge for valour specially struck at this time, in Hyde Park to those who had performed special acts of bravery during the war. It was at this time of wide distribution of honours that Her Majesty conferred upon her noble husband the title of Prince Consort. Her Majesty's ninth, and youngest, child, the Princess Beatrice, was born on the 14th of April, 1857, and no sooner does one cease to record this, the last birth in the royal household, than it becomes the pleasing duty to start with the weddings. One of the first acts of the Queen, when she had recovered from her confinement, was to announce to Parliament the formal betrothal of her daughter, the Princess Royal, to Prince Frederick William of Prussia, eldest son of the Prince and Princess of Prussia, and direct heir to the throne. Prince Fritz had visited Windsor during the Great Exhibition in 1851, and had greatly admired the young Princess at that time. When he returned in 1855, he found her "woman grown," though only fifteen years of age, and as they rode together one day among the hills of Balmoral, he declared his love by presenting the "Rose of England" with a spray of white heather. The Queen and Prince Albert gave their consent to the betrothal on condition that it was regarded, for the present, as a private family matter, the extreme youth of the Princess rendering anything more public undesirable, and the Queen felt that the marriage should not take place until her daughter had attained her seventeenth year. The two years which intervened before the Princess's marriage were clouded by the terrible incidents of the Indian Mutiny, which were a cause of continual anxiety to the Queen, and led to a "little skirmish" with Lord Palmerston. In June, 1857, the Queen was not satisfied that the Government were making sufficiently vigorous efforts to meet the crisis, and told Palmerston what she would have done had she been in the House of Commons, to which Lord Palmerston replied: "It is fortunate for those from whose opinion your Majesty differs that your Majesty is not in the House of Commons, for they would have had to encounter a formidable antagonist in argument." We find Palmerston frequently speaking at this period of the Queen's "sagacity." A few days before the marriage of her daughter the Queen addressed a beautiful letter to Sir Colin Campbell, the hero of Lucknow, and a pathetic picture of the "Relief of Lucknow" was one of the last pieces of work done by the Princess Royal before her marriage.

 This, the first wedding in the Queen's family, was attended with all the little home touches which makes Her Majesty's life so charming. She and the Prince themselves arranged the bride's presents to be viewed by their friends. The details of the marriage ceremony were identical with those of the Queen's own wedding. She calls it the "second most eventful day" in her life, and said that she felt as if she were "being married over again herself." The very youthful bride looked charming in her white silk and orange blossoms, with the famous myrtle in her bouquet, a shoot of which, planted at Osborne, has grown into a tree which supplies the royal brides of the present time. The marriage was celebrated, like the Queen's, at the Chapel Royal, St. James's Palace, and took place on the 25th of January, 1858. A pretty little scene was enacted when, as the bride advanced to the altar, the bridegroom knelt to kiss her hand. Unlike her royal mother, the young Princess had to leave home and kindred for a foreign land, and the parting, after the brief honeymoon at Windsor, was a heart-breaking one for all. The Princess had said to her mother, "I think it will kill me to say good-bye to papa"; and when the time came for her to sail for Germany, the poor young bride — clever, wilful, independent "Vicky" of the old days — was quite broken down. The Queen did not trust herself to see her daughter off, and those who saw the Prince Consort's white, rigid face as he took his last look at the departing vessel have told the present writer that they can never forget its look of sadness. When the Princess was saying good-bye to the old people about Balmoral, one old "body" up and spoke her mind to the Queen, and expressed her opinion that the Princess Royal was as sorry to leave as they were to part with her; then suddenly recollecting herself, she apologised, saying, "I mean no harm, but I always say just what I think, not what is fut" (fit). The Queen's comment on the incident was: "Dear old lady, she is such a pleasant person." Her Majesty dislikes, above everything, cringing servility, and delights in those honest, candid people who say what they think, not what is fut.

In the following August the Queen and Prince Consort visited their daughter in her new home, and the Queen was rejoiced to find her "quite the old Vicky still"; but in taking leave of her after a pleasant stay in Germany, the royal mother felt sad that it was impossible for her to return again to the young Princess at that critical time when "every other mother goes to her child." On the 27th of January, 1859, the Princess Frederick William was confined of a son, the present Emperor William, and Her Majesty found herself at thirty-nine with the ancient dignity of "grandmamma" conferred upon her. In the September of 1860 the Queen and Prince spent some time in Coburg, and were visited by "Vicky" and "Fritz" and the wonderful "baby William," who was duly brought to grandmamma's room every morning, and was pronounced "such a darling."

But the time has come when the shadow of death encompassed the life of our beloved Queen. Her mother, the Duchess of Kent, had been for some time in declining health, and in March of 1861 the Queen was summoned to Frogmore, and found her in a dying condition. She passed peacefully away, solaced by the daughter whom she had reared with unsurpassed love and care, and to whom her death came as the first great grief in life. "What a blessed end!" the Queen writes in her diary; "her gentle spirit at rest, her sufferings over! But I — I, wretched child — who had lost the mother I so tenderly loved, from whom for these forty-one years I had never been parted except for a few weeks — what was my case? My childhood — everything seemed to crowd upon me at once. I seemed to have lived through a life, to have become old!" The Queen was much depressed in the months which followed, despite the loving sympathy of her husband and children; and indeed she had not recovered her spirits when ten months later came a loss which made all others seem trivial. For the last ten years the health of the Prince Consort had been unsatisfactory; the great mental strain which he underwent in organising the Exhibition of 1851, followed by the hard work and constant anxiety attendant on the Crimean war and the Indian Mutiny, had weakened his constitution, and when in December of 1861 he was seized with an attack of typhoid fever, he had no strength to resist the disease. The agonised suspense of his wife during the fortnight which followed his seizure was in proportion to the absorbing and passionate love she had borne him throughout the twenty-one years of their wedded life. When hope was abandoned, and the doctors could no longer conceal their fears from her, the Queen writes: "I went to my room, and felt as if my heart must break." Then came a change in the Prince's condition, and the wife's heart beat fast with hope; but it was only for a few hours. As the day advanced it became evident that the Prince was sinking. Bending over him the Queen whispered, "'Tis your own little wife," and he turned his head and kissed her. After ten o'clock, on the fatal 14th of December, came the end, and the great and good Prince, who had worn, through good report and ill, "the white flower of a blameless life," passed to his reward, and the Crown was left indeed a, "lonely splendour."

THE WIDOWED MONARCH

QUEEN VICTORIA kneeling at the death-bed of her "dear lord and master," as she ever called the Prince Consort, will remain one of the most pathetic scenes in the history of this country. Queen she remained to the end, in spite of her woman's anguish. When the last sigh was heaved, and the spirit of her beloved had fled, she gently loosed the hand which she had held as he passed through the valley of the shadow of death, saw the lids closed over the eyes which to the last had turned their love-light upon her, rose from the bedside, thanked the physicians for their skill and attention, spoke some soothing words to her orphaned children sobbing around the bed, and, walking from the room calm and erect, sought the solitude of her chamber, and went through her Gethsemane alone.

Away in the city the great bell of St. Paul's tolled the sad tidings through the midnight air, and next morning — Sunday — it seemed that a pall had fallen over the land, and there was scarce a dry eye in the churches when the Prince Consort's name was significantly omitted from the Litany, and the ministers impressively paused in the prayer for "the fatherless children and widows, and all that are desolate and oppressed." To many, indeed, this was the first intimation of the great loss which the monarch and the country had sustained. As the awestruck worshippers dispersed they gathered in little knots, and spoke in whispers of the grief-stricken wife at Royal Windsor, recalled her joy-days, when, gay as a lark, she had entered the Abbey on her coronation day, or walked from the altar a proud and happy bride, and again had hung with a mother's love over the cradle of her little ones; and now, in the heyday of life and happiness she was a widowed Queen, more desolate by reason of her exalted position than any woman in the land, similarly bereft. That angel of comfort, Princess Alice, whose lovely character all the world reveres, was the support of her mother in this time of sorrow. She was aided in her ministrations by Lady Augusta Bruce (afterwards the wife of Dean Stanley), who had been the beloved friend and attendant of the Duchess of Kent in her last years; and by that other dear friend of the Queen, the Duchess of Sutherland, herself but lately a widow, who was specially summoned by her royal mistress to stay with her at this time of bereavement. Anxious days and nights were passed by these devoted ladies in the Queen's room, for the reaction from the enforced restraint had been so great that Her Majesty was completely prostrated, and her pulse became so weak at one time that death appeared imminent. It is scarcely realised to-day how near the country was to a double tragedy, and when the tidings were flashed through the land that at last the Queen had obtained some hours' sleep it seemed like the joy-bells succeeding the funeral peal. The feelings of the people were beautifully expressed by Mrs. Crosland in her poem:

"Sleep, for the night is round thee spread,
Thou daughter of a line of kings;
Sleep, widowed Queen, while angels' wings
Make canopy above thy head!
Sleep, while a million prayers rise up
To Him who knew all earthly sorrow,
That day by day each soft to-morrow
May melt the bitter from thy cup."

When the first agony of her grief was over, the Queen summoned her children around her, and told them that, though she felt crushed by her loss, she knew what her position demanded, and asked them to help her in fulfilling her duty to the country and to them. Little Prince Leopold, the delicate one of the Queen's bairns, who was at this time at Cannes for his health, when told that his father was dead, cried piteously, "Do take me to my mamma"; and that old-fashioned little tot, Baby Beatrice, would climb on her mother's knee to look at "mamma's sad cap." Fearing the worst consequences should Her Majesty have another relapse, the physicians were urgent that she should leave Windsor before the funeral took place; but the Queen cried bitterly at the suggestion, saying that her subjects never left their homes or the remains of their dear ones at such times, and why should she. It was only when Princess Alice represented to her that the younger children might suffer if they remained in the fever-tainted Castle that she consented to go with them to Osborne. Before leaving she drove to Frogmore, where only ten months before she had laid to rest her devoted mother, and walking round the gardens on the arm of Princess Alice, chose a bright sunny spot to bury her dead. The same feeling which led the Queen to create homes of her own, apart from the royal palaces, prompted her to have a family burying-place. With a truly democratic spirit, Her

Majesty preserves her own individuality, and declines to be considered a mere royalty, whose affairs are to be regulated by the State, and whose body must lie in a cold and dreary royal vault, along with kings and queens for whom she cares nothing at all. When the sad time comes, our greatest monarch will probably lie with her mother and husband in the beautiful God's acre of her own choosing. The funeral of the Prince Consort took place, with the honours befitting so great and good a Prince, on the 23rd of December, 1861, the coffin being temporarily placed at the entrance to St. George's Chapel, Windsor, until the beautiful mausoleum had been built at Frogmore; upon the lid were laid wreaths of green moss and violets, made by the Queen and Princess Alice. The unmistakable reality of the sorrow at the funeral was very striking, and was manifested, not only by the heart-broken sobs of the young Princes, but by the tears of veteran statesmen and ambassadors mingling with those who were of royal kin. Though there can be no doubt that the Prince had won for himself a place in the hearts of those present, one feels that the tears flowed as much in sympathy for her who sorrowed as for him who was gone. In reading the letters and memoirs of courtiers of this period, it is evident that they felt that the Queen had well-nigh received her death-blow; all speak of her calm, pathetic sorrow being heart breaking to witness. Amongst others, Lord Shaftesbury writes at this time: "The desolation of the Queen's heart and life, the death-blow to her happiness on earth! God in His mercy sustain and comfort! The disruption of domestic existence, unprecedented in royal history, the painful withdrawal of a prop, the removal of a counsellor, a friend in all public and private affairs, the sorrows she has, the troubles that await her — all rend my heart as though the suffering were my own."

Her Majesty spent the first three months of her widowhood in absolute retirement at Osborne, where she was greatly comforted by her beloved half-sister, the Princess Hohenlohe, who had hastened from Germany to her side. The Princess told Dean Stanley that the Queen found "her only comfort in the belief that her husband's spirit was close beside her — for he had promised her that it should be so"; and she further related that the Queen would go each morning to visit the cows on the Prince's model farm, because he used to do it, and she fancied the gentle creatures would miss him. King Leopold of Belgium, ever Her Majesty's support and counsellor, as he had been that of her widowed mother, was also at Osborne at this time; but even with near and trusted relations certain reserve and etiquette had to be observed by the Queen, and one can understand the bitterness of her cry, "There is no one left to call me 'Victoria' now." Mother and husband had both been taken within a year, and the old royal family, those elderly aunts and uncles who had been about her in her youth, were passing one by one into the silent land. The

Prince of Wales was not of an age to take any responsible position, and shortly after his father's death set out, in accordance with the Prince Consort's plans, which the Queen would not have put on one side, for a prolonged tour in the East, accompanied by Arthur Penrhyn Stanley (Dean of Westminster). The Queen's eldest daughter was bound by the ties of her German home, and it was therefore upon Princess Alice that everything devolved during those first terrible weeks. The nation has never forgotten the tact and judgment in dealing with Ministers and officials, in the Queen's place, shown by this young girl of eighteen, and her remarkable conduct called forth a special article in the Times.

The advocates of modern funeral reform might complain that Her Majesty was too punctilious in her outward signs of mourning; but, as she once playfully said to Lord Melbourne in her young days, "What is the use of being a queen if you cannot do as you like?" It is said that she refused to sign a Commission because the paper was not bordered with black; and we know that for at least eight years after the Prince Consort's death the royal servants wore a band of crape upon the left arm, while in her own attire Her Majesty has never, throughout the succeeding years of her widowhood, worn any but mourning colours. So complete was her isolation during her retirement at Osborne that she dined alone save for one of the royal children, who took it in turns to be with her, the other members of the family and the visitors, even her uncle Leopold, dining separately. At her command the late Prince's apartments at Windsor, Osborne, and Balmoral were closed, and remain to-day exactly as they were at his death. His favourite horse, Guy Mannering, was turned out to a life of ease in Bushey Park, the saddle never again being placed upon his back; while the memory of his favourite dog, Eos, which predeceased him, was preserved on the Prince's tomb, where the faithful greyhound is sculptured at his master's feet. This dog accompanied the Prince when he came to be married; and his brother, Duke Ernest, tells the story that as he and Prince Albert passed through a little German town on their way to England in 1839, the country people came out to see them, and Prince Albert for a "lark" put his little black greyhound up at the carriage window for the people to stare at, while he and his brother, convulsed with laughter, crouched down in the bottom of the carriage out of sight. Not only were the Prince's rooms preserved in the state in which he left them — a custom which the Queen follows with all her nearest departed relatives — but her own boudoir at Windsor Castle is kept in the same state to-day as it was when the Prince Consort died. On the door is inscribed, "Every article in this room my lamented husband selected for me in the twenty-fourth year of my reign." In this room the Queen's bridal wreath and the first bouquet which the Prince presented to her lie withered in a glass case.

She wasted no time in idle tears, and a simple little incident occurred at the time which showed that some of Her Majesty's old interest in life was returning. When out driving in the neighbourhood of Windsor one afternoon, she was attracted by a poor Italian vendor of images, and ordering the carriage to be stopped, astonished the man by buying up a large portion of his stock-in-trade; but still greater must have been his surprise when it transpired that neither the Queen nor her suite had sufficient cash to pay for the purchases. However, matters were eventually arranged to the perfect satisfaction of the man with the images, who doubtless ever afterwards dubbed himself, "By Appointment."

Nowhere has the Queen such a sense of quiet and homeliness as at Balmoral, where, amongst her faithful Highlanders, she lives on terms of mutual aid and sympathy which recall the Scottish laird among his clansmen, and it would seem that, like Sir Walter Scott, she cannot live a year without a sight of the heather. Up to the time of her bereavement she had only stayed there in the autumn, when the Prince was deer-stalking; but the year after his death she began the custom, since continued, of spending her own birthday in May, and that of the Prince in August, in the Highland home endeared to her by so many memories of the dead. The first visit paid by the Queen when she went there in the spring of 1862 was to an old cottager, who like herself had lately lost her husband, and the two widows, so differently placed in life, mingled their tears together. The old woman apologised for indulging her grief; but the Queen told her that she "was so thankful to cry with some one who knew exactly how she felt." Her Majesty is always a Scotchwoman when she is at her Highland home, and during this time of sorrow, in characteristic Scotch fashion, the first thing she did was to send for the minister. It was to the Rev. Dr. Norman Macleod that she appealed for religious guidance, and deeply grateful was she for his faithful counsel. When he pointed out to her the duty of resignation to the divine Will, she received his admonitions very sweetly, and sent him a touching letter of thanks. Dr. Macleod afterwards wrote: "I am never tempted to conceal any conviction from the Queen, for I feel she sympathises with what is true, and likes the speaker to utter the truth exactly as he believes it." Her Majesty was first attracted by Dr. Macleod's preaching in 1854, when he was officiating at Crathic Church, and the references in his prayer to herself and her children gave her, as she says, a "lump in her throat." Later in the day Her Majesty and Prince Albert were taking their usual evening stroll, when they encountered the minister sitting on a block of granite in quiet meditation. The Queen at once advanced towards him and thanked him for his sermon, and the conversation which followed was the beginning of a friendship which ended only with Dr. Macleod's death. He was constantly at Balmoral during the Queen's early widowhood; in fact, it would seem that Her Majesty could hardly get on without him. She asked not only his spiritual guidance, but made him her confidant in matters relating to the training of her children, as she perpetually felt the responsibility of being a widow with a large family. "No one," she said, "ever reassured and comforted me about my children like Dr. Macleod." At times he turned entertainer for Her Majesty, and would read Burns and Scott to her as she sat spinning. In this homely occupation the Queen is proficient, having taken her first lessons from an old woman at Balmoral, who for many years had in her possession flax spun by Her Majesty, until it was begged away thread by thread by enterprising tourists. The Queen has an interesting collection of spinning-wheels, and has sent specimens of her work to exhibitions. It is interesting to find from Dr. Macleod that her favourite poem from Burns was, "A man's a man for a' that." This, however, is but further evidence of Her Majesty's democratic sentiments, which are very evident, notwithstanding her imperial spirit, which brooks no encroachment upon her authority as a constitutional sovereign.

In the course of his talks with the Queen, Dr Macleod told her of an old Scotchwoman, who had lost her husband and several children, and had had many sorrows, but when asked how she could bear them said: "When he was taen, it made sic a hole in my heart that a'other sorrows gang lichtly through." "So will it ever be with me," was the Queen's remark when she heard the story. One imagines that there was something of the feeling that one loss more could make her loneliness little greater, in the Queen's consenting to part with her beloved daughter Princess Alice, who had been betrothed to Prince Louis of Hesse before her father's death, and whose marriage and removal to Germany took place in the July following. Painful indeed is the contrast between the marriages of the Queen's two eldest daughters: the one a joyous repetition of the gay ceremonies which attended her own bridal, and the second performed privately at Osborne in a scene of partial mourning, when everybody cried, even to the Archbishop. The sweet young Princess, whom her father called "the beauty of the family," looked pathetically lovely in her dress of crystalline silk, trimmed with Honiton flounces made from a design chosen by the Prince Consort. She was given away by her paternal uncle, Duke Ernest of Coburg, the Queen sitting in deep mourning in the background of the bridal party. There was no wedding breakfast, but after the ceremony the young couple lunched privately with the Queen and "Baby," as Princess Beatrice was yet called. This was indeed the "sad marriage" in the royal family.

The following month Her Majesty was again at Balmoral, where she erected the Cairn to the Prince Consort on the Craig Lowrigan. "I and my poor six orphans," she writes, "all placed stones on it, and our initials, as well as those of the three absent ones." Below the inscription is the beautiful motto from the Apocrypha chosen by the Princess Royal:

*"He being made perfect in a short time fulfilled a long time;
For his soul pleased the Lord.
Therefore hastened He to take him away from among the wicked."*

During the first years of her widowhood the Queen could not bear to listen to music, still less to take part in its performance, which had hitherto been such a delight to her; neither did she feel able to amuse herself with her favourite pastime of sketching. Mr. Leitch, the artist, who was drawing-master to the Queen and royal family for twenty-two years, describes in a letter to his mother the sadly altered life at Balmoral at this period. He writes: "The Queen is still the kind, good, gracious lady that she always was; but I need hardly tell you that there is a change. Indeed the whole place is changed. Everything very quiet and still. How different from my first visit here — the joyous bustle in the morning when the Prince went out; the Highland ponies and the dogs; the gillies and the pipers coming home; the Queen and her ladies going out to meet them; and the merry time afterwards; the torchlight sword dances on the green, and the servants' ball closing." In the following autumn Her Majesty was persuaded to resume sketching, and Mr. Leitch gives a graphic account of an outdoor drawing-party. The Queen set out on her Highland pony led by John Brown, Lady Jane Churchill, one of the ladies-in-waiting to whom the Queen was specially attached during this period of loneliness, walking alongside the pony, the Princess Louise and Mr. Leitch trudging along the road together after them. When the place selected for sketching was reached, the Queen seated herself in the middle of the country road, with a rough stone from the Dee as a rest for her paint-box, Lady Churchill holding an umbrella to shade the Queen's eyes. Princess Louise sat on a stone a little farther away, while Mr. Leitch attended the party as instructor, and John Brown looked after the pony. The country folk stared in astonishment as they passed by, and Her Majesty heartily enjoyed the fun, and seemed to revive a little of her lost animation. She sketched for two hours, and then remarked how quickly time passed when she was drawing, and expressed her determination to do more of it. So in her second loneliness the Queen found consolation in the use of pencil and brush, as she had done in her rather dull and monotonous childhood.

At the marriage of the Prince of Wales with the Princess Alexandra of Denmark in St. George's Chapel, Windsor, on the 10th of March, 1863, the Queen sat apart in her grief, unable to mingle in the gay festivity. It was after the birth of a son to the young couple in January, 1864, that she gave the first sign of returning interest in public life, and commanded that in honour of the event her birthday in the succeeding May should be celebrated in London with the trooping of the colours and general festivities, which had been suspended since the death of the Prince Consort. The people were, however, disappointed in the hope that Her Majesty was going to resume her old place in society, and indeed the charming manner in which her son's wife was taking her place seemed to render it unnecessary, especially when the Queen was already overburdened with governmental work, the care of her younger children, and the management of her vast estates. From glimpses one gets into Her Majesty's home life of this period, it would seem that "Baby" Beatrice was a very amusing little person. She was fond of experimenting in the cooking line, and having manufactured some confectionery, which appears to have been so fearfully and wonderfully made that her friends declined to taste it, she said philosophically, "Never mind; I will give it to the donkey, as Dean Stanley is not here," the little Princess being aware that the Dean had neither taste nor smell, and was therefore an undiscriminating person regarding pasties. The Princess Louise had the reputation of being the best cook among the royal children, and we find her coming to the rescue on one of the Queen's Highland expeditions, when the luggage had broken down on the way, and making her mother some delicious coffee. The story comes from Balmoral that Princesses Helena and Louise called one day, as was customary for them, to ask one of the cottage children to come and play with them; the mother replied that her daughter must finish baking some oatcakes first. "Oh, we'll help," volunteered the Princess Louise, and not being able to lay her hands on the cutter, she seized the teapot lid in her anxiety to get the business over, and succeeded in getting the unfortunate cakes into such a sticky, misshapen mess that the guid wife promptly despatched her daughter with her over-officious visitors and finished the baking herself.

An amusing incident is told of the Queen's third son, Prince Arthur, when he was at the Ranger's Lodge, Blackheath, pursuing his military studies. His sister's former governess, Miss Hillyard, was staying for her health in the neighbourhood, and each morning he was in the habit of walking to her house to inquire how she was, and in doing so passed by the apple-stall of an old Irishwoman, named Kitty, who from his cadet's dress took him for a private in the artillery. One day she asked a policeman if he could tell her who "that 'tillery chap" was that passed by every day, adding, "He looks such a graceful, nice young man, that I'm sorry in my heart to see him as he is, for I'm shure he comes of dacent people, he looks so genteel, and I be always thinking, shure, if his people is anyway well off, isn't it a wonder they don't buy him out." One can imagine old Kitty's eloquence when she was informed that he was the Queen's son.

In February, 1866, Her Majesty emerged from her long seclusion to open Parliament in person, and the occasion was one of great splendour and interest, remarkable for the numerous assemblage of ladies present in the House of Lords; in fact, the array of peeresses filling the back rows of seats behind the peers, as well as the side galleries and the great gallery, might have led a stranger to suppose that women had at length been admitted to Parliament. At noon the streets recalled the palmy days of the Queen's wedded life; crowds of spectators lined the route to Westminster, and a long line of carriages filled with ladies in full-dress stretched from Pall Mall to the Peers' entrance. Before the appearance of Her Majesty, the Princess of Wales, looking lovely in a white tulle dress trimmed with black lace, was conducted to a seat on the woolsack, facing the throne, whereon was spread the State robes which the Queen had no heart to wear. It was a moment of thrilling and pathetic interest when Her Majesty entered, dressed in a robe of deep violet velvet, trimmed with ermine, and wearing a white lace cap, a la Marie Stuart, with a gauze veil flowing behind; her dress, indeed, gave her a remarkable likeness to the unfortunate Queen of Scots. She was accompanied by the Princesses Helena and Louise, dressed in half-mourning costumes, and escorted to her seat by the Prince of Wales. She sat with downcast eyes, looking very grave and sad, while the speech from the throne, which in happier days had been delivered by her with such rare elocutionary power, was read by the Lord Chamberlain. One feels that the occasion was a little trying for Princess Helena, as the formal announcement was made of her approaching marriage with Prince Christian of Schleswig-Holstein.

In the March following the Queen reviewed the troops at Aldershot, and both this and the opening of Parliament by her gave the greatest pleasure, not only to the nation, but to the Queen's own family, and Princess Alice wrote to tell her mother how happy she was that she had made "the great effort." "How trying," she says, "the visit to Aldershot must have been; but it is so wise and kind of you to go. I cannot think of it without tears in my eyes. Formerly that was one of the greatest pleasures of my girlhood, and you and darling papa looked so handsome together." During the same year the Queen attended two weddings, that of the Princess Mary of Cambridge and the Duke of Teck, which took place at Kew on the 12th of June, 1866, and that of the Princess Helena and Prince Christian, which was celebrated at Windsor on the following 5th of July, the Queen giving away the bride. At the close of this year the growing discontent of the people that Her Majesty showed no disposition to resume her old place in Court functions was made the occasion of public demonstration at a meeting at St. James's

Hall, in support of the enfranchisement of the working classes, when Mr. Ayrton, M.P., condemned the Queen's retirement in strong terms. This brought John Bright to his feet, who warmly vindicated Her Majesty from Mr. Ayrton's charge that she had neglected her duty to society. "I am not accustomed," said Mr. Bright, "to stand up in defence of those who are the possessors of crowns, but I feel that there has been a great injustice done to the Queen, and I venture to say this, that a woman — be she the queen of a great realm or the wife of one of your labouring men — who can keep alive in her heart a great sorrow for the lost object of her life and affection, is not at all likely to be wanting in a great and generous sympathy with you." As the great orator ceased, a remarkable ovation took place, the entire audience rising and singing "God Save the Queen" with every demonstration of love and loyalty. When two years later the name of John Bright was submitted to Her Majesty for a seat in Mr. Gladstone's Cabinet, she expressed her pleasure, saying that she was under the greatest obligation to him for the many kind words he had spoken of her, and despatched a special messenger to tell Mr. Bright that if it was more agreeable to his feelings as a Quaker to omit the ceremony of kneeling and kissing hands, he was at liberty to do so, of which permission Mr. Bright availed himself. The Princess Royal was present during his reception at Windsor, and told him that both herself and all the members of the royal family were greatly indebted to him for the way in which he had spoken of their mother. Mr. Bright has recorded his estimate of the Queen's character to the effect that she was the "most absolutely straightforward and truthful person" he had ever known.

VICTORIA, QUEEN AND EMPRESS

FAR away in sunny India was enacted, on the 1st of January, 1877, a scene the most brilliant and unique of any connected with the glorious reign of Victoria. At the Imperial Camp, outside the walls of Delhi, where the Mutiny had raged the fiercest, Her Majesty was proclaimed Empress of India. On a throne of Oriental splendour, above which was the portrait of the Empress, sat Lord Lytton, her Viceroy; the Governors, Lieutenants, State officials and the Maharajahs, Rajahs, Nabobs, and Princes, with their glittering retinues grouped around him. Behind rose the vast amphitheatre, filled with foreign ambassadors and notables, around was the concourse of spectators and a brilliant array of fifteen thousand troops, while to complete the gorgeous scene the whole assemblage was surrounded by an unbroken chain of elephants decked with gay trappings. After the Proclamation had been made with all the pomp of heraldry, the Viceroy presented to each of the feudatory Princes the Empress's gift, a magnificent standard, made by Messrs. Elkington, after a design chosen by Her Majesty. The standards were ornamented with the sacred water lily of India, spreading palms of the East, and the rose of England, it being the desire of the Empress to indicate that as the rose and lily intertwined beneath the spreading palm, so was the welfare of India to become one with that of her older dominions; and the motto, "Heaven's light our guide," illustrated the spirit in which she desired to govern the enormous empire of which she ever fondly speaks as "a bright jewel in her crown." Most noticeable in the brilliant gathering was the Begum of Bhopal, a lady Knight of the Most Noble Order of Queen Victoria. There was nothing to be seen of the lady save a bundle of floating azure silk, which indicated that she was inside, and upon the place where the left shoulder was supposed to be was emblazoned the shield of the Star of India. Much cheap wit was expended after Her Majesty's accession on the rise of the "royal sex," and it was said that the young Queen intended to establish an Order of Female Knighthood. The prophecy of the scoffer seemed to have been more than fulfilled in the figure of this Hindoo lady wearing the Order of the Star of India. Though she was not valiant enough to show her face, yet her presence was a good omen for that emancipation of the women of her country from the seclusion of the Zenana which is fittingly distinguishing the reign of the British Empress. On the day of the Proclamation at Delhi, the Queen conferred the Grand Cross of India upon the Duke of Connaught, and when in 1879 she became a great-grandmother, by the birth of a daughter to the Princess of Saxe-Meiningen (Princess Charlotte of Prussia), she celebrated her ancient dignity by investing twelve noble ladies of her Court with the Imperial Order of the Crown of India.

The keenest interest has always been shown by the Queen in the condition of Hindoo women. It was with heartfelt thankfulness that she saw the barbarous suttee abolished, and it was her influence which inspired the rapid spread of Zenana work. In July, 1881, she received at Windsor Miss Beilby, a medical missionary from India; and after listening to her account of the sufferings of Hindoo women, in time of illness, for need of doctors, the Queen turned to her ladies and said, "We had no idea that things were as bad as this." Miss Beilby then took from a locket which she wore round her neck a folded piece of paper containing a message to Her Majesty from the Maharanee of Poonah. "The women of India suffer when they are sick," was the burden of the dark-eyed Queen's appeal. The Empress returned her a message of sympathy and help, and to the women of our own land the Queen said, "We desire it to be generally known that we sympathise with every effort made to relieve the suffering state of the women of India"; and when Lord Dufferin went out as Governor-General, she commissioned Lady Dufferin to establish a permanent fund for providing qualified women doctors for work in India. Her Majesty continues to take the greatest interest in this work, and is in constant communication with the Viceroy's wife regarding its further organisation and extension.

No opportunity is lost by Her Majesty to show her interest in her Indian Empire, and doubtless had the Prince Consort been spared she would have made a progress through the country. This was done in her stead by the Prince of Wales in 1875-6, and it was while he was making the tour that Lord Beaconsfield introduced the Royal Titles Bill into Parliament, conferring upon the Queen the title of Empress of India, a distinction regarded by John Bull as superfluous to a Crown the most distinguished in the world; but Her Majesty personally desired it, not, as gossip affirmed, because of the advent at Court of her second son's imperial bride, but as a means of binding her Indian subjects to her in a closer manner. It is said that she showed more interest in the Indian Court of the Colonial

Exhibition, 1886, than in any other, and at each of her visits chatted freely with the native workmen. When the Indian delegates to the Exhibition first saw their Empress, a homely-looking lady in a black silk gown, they expressed disappointment, having expected to see her decked out in the pomp and circumstance of a mighty potentate. "But, after all," said they, "what a great power the Queen must wield when she can command such an array of illustrious personages to attend upon her, while she appears as the most simple of all the Court." Of late years Her Majesty has had Indian servants in native dress as personal attendants; she is also an assiduous student of Hindustani, being able to speak and write in that language; and her favourite State jewel is the priceless Koh-i-noor, about which hangs a tale. When it came into the possession of the East India Company, in 1850, it was handed at a Board meeting to John Lawrence (afterwards Lord Lawrence, the Viceroy) for safe keeping. The precious diamond was laid amongst folds of linen in a small box, and Lord Lawrence slipped it into his waistcoat pocket, and forgot all about it until some days later it was suggested that he should forward it to the Queen. One can imagine his consternation when he rushed to his house to see if it was to be found. "Have you seen a small box in one of my waistcoat pockets?" he asked breathlessly of his servant. "Yes, sahib," was the reply. "I found it, and put it in one of your boxes." "Bring it here and open it, and see what it contains," said his master. "There is nothing in it, sahib, but a bit of glass," the man replied in wonderment. The "bit of glass" was in due course despatched to the Queen, whose crown it was to adorn; but she has preferred to wear it on occasions as a magnificent brooch in the centre of her bodice. The cutting of the diamond was personally superintended by the Prince Consort. It is always kept at Windsor, a facsimile being in the royal crown at the Tower.

An interesting event in the Queen's family circle took place in February, 1871, when at St. George's Chapel, Windsor, she gave away her clever, handsome daughter Princess Louise to the heir of the Argyles. The Queen has constantly testified her regard for the old Scottish nobility by visiting their castles. She stayed for the first time as the guest of the Duke of Argyle at Inverary in 1847, and this interesting note about her future son-in-law occurs in her "Journal": "The pipers walked before the carriage, and the Highlanders on either side as we approached the house. Outside stood the Marquis of Lorne, just two years old, a dear, white, fat little fellow with reddish hair, but very delicate features, like both his father and mother; he is such a merry, independent little child." In the years which followed, Her Majesty had other opportunities for observing Lord Lorne; but before she consented to the betrothal of her daughter she consulted "the minister," and was assured by Dr. Macleod that he had a high opinion of the young

Marquis. A gentleman who saw the festivities at the home-coming of the newly wedded pair to Inverary has told the present writer that the bride's dancing at the Tenants' Ball made quite a sensation — she "footed it" in the reels and strathspeys in a way which did credit to the wife of a Highland chief. Three years later came the marriage of Prince Alfred to the Grand Duchess Marie of Russia, at St. Petersburg, which was the first and only wedding in her family at which the Queen was not present; but she commissioned her dear friends Dean Stanley and his wife, Lady Augusta, to convey her maternal greetings and little private gifts to the bride, and was most anxious that her Russian daughter-in-law should wear myrtle in her bridal attire. Myrtle is the German marriage emblem, and Her Majesty is most particular that all the royal brides shall wear it along with their orange blossoms.

During this period the hand of death was laid on many of the Queen's loved ones. Her uncle Leopold, good old Baron Stockmar, and her beloved half-sister the Princess Hohenlohe, had all passed away, and the life of her eldest son had hung by a thread in December, 1871, but the greatest loss of all came with the death of Princess Alice. The pathetic story of the Princess's devoted nursing of her husband and little ones when they were attacked with diphtheria at Darmstadt is well remembered, and when she succumbed to the disease herself it was felt than she would never rally. Princess Christian says that her sister Alice had never really recovered from the fearful shock she received in 1873, when her little boy Fritz fell from a top window, and was dashed to the ground before the eyes of his agonised mother. Visits to the Queen at Osborne or Balmoral would revive her spirits and bring back the roses to her cheeks, but only for a time. The end came on the anniversary of her father's death, the fatal 14th of December, 1878. Almost the last thing she did was to read a letter from her mother, which Sir William Jenner, who had been despatched by the Queen, had brought. It seemed as though her spirit had been lingering for this message from home, and laying it beside her she said, "Now I will fall asleep"; but it was the sleep of death upon which she entered. Her last request to her husband was that the dear old English flag might be placed upon her coffin, and she hoped that the people of her adopted country would not mind. The life of Princess Alice had been singularly beautiful, and like that of her elder sister, the Empress Frederick, full of high endeavour on behalf of her sex. It was a consolation to the Queen to gather the motherless children from Darmstadt around her at Osborne, where they completed their convalescence, and in the early spring she took one of those Continental trips from which she always receives much benefit. This year she travelled incognita as the Countess of Balmoral, and spent a month at the Villa Clara, charmingly situated at Baveno, near Lake

Maggiore, where she made informal excursions in the district, accompanied by Princess Beatrice.

The Egyptian campaign of 1882 was a period of great anxiety to the Queen, and recalled the days of the Crimean war. She received the news of the victory of Tel-el-Kebir when at Balmoral, and ordered a bonfire to be lighted on Craig Gowan, as had been done at the fall of Sebastopol twenty-one years before. In the earlier war she regretted she had not a son old enough for service; but now with the tidings of Tel-el-Kebir came Sir Garnet Wolseley's telegram that her soldier-son, the Duke of Connaught, had "behaved admirably, leading his brigade to the attack." His young wife, Princess Louise of Prussia, to whom he had been married in March, 1879, was staying at Balmoral at the time; and the Queen, with characteristic impulse, hastened with the telegram to her daughter-in-law's room, and, embracing her, wept together with her for joy that their beloved one was safe and so much praised. On the same auspicious day Her Majesty welcomed home her youngest son, the Duke of Albany, with his bride, Princess Helen of Waldeck; and the rejoicings at Balmoral in honour of the double events were exceptionally hearty.

In time of war the Queen's first thought is for the sick and wounded, and now she took an early opportunity to visit Netley Hospital, an institution which owes its existence to her initiative, and which she has always watched over with maternal care. It was the first public place which she visited after her husband's death, and she was greatly touched by a dying soldier lifting his eyes to her and saying, "I thank God that He has allowed me to live long enough to see your Majesty with my own eyes." During another visit she talked with a man who had been shot through the lungs at Lucknow. It was the Queen's custom after going the round of the wards to visit the married quarters for the accommodation of the wives and children of the patients in the hospital, and the women received an agreeable surprise when the Queen looked in upon them in the midst of their household occupations. After the Egyptian campaign she delighted the inmates by the gift of five knitted quilts, one being entirely her own work, and it bore the royal crown and the initials "V. R." in the corner; another was knitted by Princess Beatrice, and marked with her initials; while the remaining three were worked by ladies of the Court, a border being added to each by the Queen's own hands. We fancy there must have been some difficulty at Netley in deciding who was to have the honour of sleeping under the Queen's quilt. At this time Her Majesty testified her regard for the noble band of nurses by establishing the Order of the Red Cross for Ladies. The installation took place at Windsor, when the Princess of Wales and Princess Beatrice were the first names enrolled, and ten lady nurses received the honour for their services in the Zulu and Egyptian campaigns.

We cannot pass away from this period of the Queen's life without a reference to her literary activities and the delight she took in the society of men of letters, as evinced by the fact that her most frequent visitors were Dean Stanley, Sir Arthur Helps, and Sir Theodore Martin. Sir Arthur Helps edited her "Journal in the Highlands"; Sir Theodore Martin was for seven years engaged upon the "Life of the Prince Consort," under the Queen's direction; and Dean Stanley was frequently the vade mecum for enabling her to informally meet literary celebrities. Carlyle, in a letter to his sister, the late Mrs. Aitken, of Dumfries, thus describes his meeting the Queen at Dean Stanley's in 1869: "The Stanleys and we were all in a flow of talk, and some flunkeys had done setting coffee-pots and tea-cups of a sublime pattern, when Her Majesty, punctual to the minute, glided in, escorted by her dame-in-waiting (a Duchess of Athol) and by the Princess Louise, decidedly a very pretty young lady, and clever too, as I found out in talking to her afterwards. The Queen came softly forward, a kindly smile on her face, gently shook hands with all the three women, gently acknowledged with a nod the silent bows of us male monsters; and directly in her presence every one was at ease again. She is a comely little lady, with a pair of kind, clear, and intelligent grey eyes; still looks almost young (in 'spite of one broad wrinkle which shows on each cheek occasionally); is still plump; has a fine, low voice, soft; indeed, her whole manner is melodiously perfect. It is impossible to imagine a politer little woman; nothing the least imperious; all gentle, all sincere, looking unembarrassing — rather attractive, even; makes you feel, too (if you have any sense in you), that she is Queen." On this occasion Robert Browning, Sir Charles Lyell, and Grote the historian were present; and with each the Queen had her little say, and made inquiries as to the work upon which they were engaged. A year later Dickens was commanded to Windsor, and he was most struck by the simple naivete of the Queen's manner and her acquaintance with literature. The works of George Eliot were a constant source of pleasure to her; and it need hardly be said that she admired the author of "Idylls of the King," the dedication of which remains the most beautiful tribute to her husband's memory. She paid a visit to Tennyson at Freshwater, as she did to Lord Beaconsfield at Hughenden, although she appreciated the latter more as a statesman than as a litterateur. She sent her three sons to attend his funeral, and a wreath of primroses was laid upon the coffin with the inscription, "His favourite flowers, from Osborne; a tribute of affection from Queen Victoria." In short, Her Majesty prides herself upon having personally known most of the famous authors of her reign, from Wordsworth to Tennyson, and she is not without appreciation for the rising school.

Simple confidence in her readers is shown in her Highland Journals, in which the little incidents of her family life in Scotland are so frankly told. Apart from the interest attaching to the royal author, the books are of value for the graphic sketches which they contain of Highland life and scenery. Whether it be a christening, a wedding, a burial, or a sheep-clipping, the celebration of the Sacrament at Crathic Church, a torchlight dance, or the festival of Halloween, it is described as it passed before the writer's eyes, and leaves upon the reader an impression lasting and vivid. Specially interesting is the author's description of Scott's country and Abbotsford, where she had tea in the room in which the novelist died, and lingered about the study where he wrote. When requested that she should inscribe her name in his journal, she replied that "it would be a presumption for her to do so," but finally yielded to the wish of those present. Equally entertaining is her account of Prince Charlie's country, through which, curiously enough, she was conducted by Cameron of Lochiel, whose great-grand-uncle was the real moving cause of the rebellion of '45 to dethrone Her Majesty's great-great-grandfather. "Yes," she writes, "I feel a sort of reverence in going over these scenes in this most beautiful country, which I am proud to call my own, where there was such devoted loyalty to the family of my ancestors — for Stuart blood is in my veins, and I am now their representative, and the people are as devoted and loyal to me as they were to that unhappy race." The demand for the Queen's "Highland Journal" was enormous. It is said that the circulating libraries ordered it by the ton, and the press swarmed with reviews, which the royal author read with great interest, although we fancy the spice of the experience was lost by the previous overlooking of the reviews by the ladies-in-waiting. The proceeds of the sales were devoted to establishing bursaries, male and female, in the parish school of Crathie and the Queen's Schools at Girnock. The dedication of the second volume, "More Leaves," by the Queen to her "Loyal Highlanders, and especially to her devoted personal attendant and faithful friend, John Brown," was the cause of much comment. This instance of a mighty queen and empress dedicating her book to a servant is unique in literature; but Her Majesty regards a faithful servant as an honoured friend, and one of the most beautiful traits in her character is that she never forgets those who serve her. Honest John was as plain-spoken as he was faithful, and the story is told in Deeside that one day, when the Queen was out, she desired to sketch, and asked for a table to be borrowed from a neighbouring cottage. There was great difficulty in finding one of the right height; table after table was returned, and the eager people were in despair at not being able to suit the royal requirements. At length John Brown seized hold of the most likely one of the discarded tables, and setting it down before his royal mistress, said with irresistible logic, "They canna mak' one on purpose for you," at which the Queen laughed, and settled down to her sketching. Brown had his eye, too, on his mistress's appearance, and did she come out in a warm comfortable garment a little antiquated in cut, he would remark, "What's that you've got on the day?" Despite his brusqueness, the faithful fellow would have stood between the Queen and a bullet any day, and indeed anxiety for her safety caused his death. During the years 1881-2 attempts had been made upon the Queen's life on two occasions, and she was feeling nervous with regard to the Fenian outrages, when a great scare was created in Windsor by Lady Florence Dixie declaring that she had been attacked by Fenians in the grounds of her house, not far from the Castle. So anxious was Her Majesty that she sent John Brown to explore the shrubberies of Lady Florence Dixie's house, and in doing so he took a chill, which resulted in his death, on the 27th of March, 1883, after three days' illness. His royal mistress gave orders that his body should be conveyed to his native Highlands for burial. The grave can be soon by the visitor to Crathie churchyard, along with that of Francie Clark, who succeeded Brown as Her Majesty's personal attendant, and died a short time ago. Inside the church a monument was erected to his memory by "his grateful and affectionate sovereign and friend, Victoria R.I.," with the inscription, "Kings love him that speaketh right." Apropos of the Queen's kindness to her servants, a story was lately told the writer by a gentleman acquainted with the girl to whom it relates. She was one of the housemaids at Balmoral, and the Queen, chancing to meet her on the staircase one day, saw that she had been crying, and asked the reason of her grief. Seeing that the girl was reluctant to speak, Her Majesty commanded her to come to her private sitting-room, and there tell her what was the matter. The girl reluctantly explained that she had received notice to leave because she objected to attending the Established Kirk along with the rest of the Balmoral servants. Upon hearing this, the Queen sent for the head of her household, and desired that the housemaid in question should have her notice withdrawn, and that in future no one in her service should be persecuted on account of their religious views.

The death of John Brown came at a time when the Queen was suffering severely from a fall on one of the staircases at Windsor Castle, which sprained her knees and crippled her for several weeks; and in the following year, before she had recovered her health and spirits, she was smitten by a still heavier blow in the death of her youngest son, Prince Leopold, suddenly at Cannes, whither he had gone for a change. Delicate health had inclined him to cultured, scholarly studies, and he was more like the Prince Consort than any of the Queen's sons, and to him she was beginning to look as the one fitted to perform the delicate duty of private secretary in the place of him whom she had lost. The sad news was broken to her at Osborne by the late Sir Henry Ponsonby, and, though quite prostrated by it, she was, as ever, thoughtful of others, and desired Princess Beatrice to leave her side and hasten to comfort the young widow at Claremont, whose delicate condition rendered the shock of the tidings more serious. The Empress Eugenie, who was staying near Osborne, came to the Queen to offer consolation, and after spending some hours with her was able to report that Her Majesty was greatly relieved by being able to talk over her loss with one who knew what bereavement was. Some years before the positions had been reversed, and it was the Queen who had comforted the Empress, first, after the death of the exiled Emperor, and again when her only son met such a terrible death in the Zulu war of 1879. Prince Leopold, like his father, had premonitions of death. "He would talk to me about death," writes one who was with him a few days before he died, "and said he would like a military funeral." I asked, "Why, sir, do you talk in this melancholy manner?" As he was about to answer he was called away, and said, "I'll tell you later." I never saw him again, but he finished his answer to me, to another lady, and said: "For two nights now Princess Alice has appeared to me in my dreams, and says she is quite happy, and that she wants me to come and join her." The body of the Prince was brought from Cannes and interred at St. George's, Windsor.

In 1885, the year following Prince Leopold's death, came the last marriage in the Queen's family, that of "Baby" Beatrice, who had now for fourteen years been her mother's devoted attendant, to the late Prince Henry of Battenberg. Princess Beatrice, having been so much with grown-up people when a child, was a little quaint in her ways, and several stories are told of her funny little speeches. When a little lady of six she found it very difficult to get proper respect shown her by her nephew and niece of Germany, and taking Dr. Macleod into her confidence, she said: "What do you think, Dr. Macleod? I am an aunt, and yet my nephew William won't do what I bid him. Both he and Elizabeth refused to shut the door! Is that not naughty?" The wedding of the Queen's youngest daughter took place from Osborne at the little ivy-clad village church of Whippingham. Only semi-State was observed. The bride wore her mother's Honiton lace and veil, and was attended by her ten young nieces in white tulle frocks. Little children strewed flowers and decked the wayside with homely tributes of affection, and the whole scene was an ideally perfect village wedding. It was arranged that the bride should continue to live with her mother as Princess in waiting. The marriage proved one of great happiness, and in her new son-in-law Her Majesty found one who joined with his wife in unselfish ministrations to her comfort. His untimely death was a real personal loss, as well as grief to the Queen.

Although it had long been apparent that Her Majesty would never again resume her old place in society, she had during the past ten years officiated at a number of public ceremonials, and had held occasional drawing-rooms, as well as now and again re-opening Parliament, and in May of 1886 she opened the Colonial and Indian Exhibition at South Kensington. This notable ceremony, which vividly recalled to her the Exhibition of '51, seemed like a gathering together of the representatives from all parts of her mighty empire as a prelude to the celebration of her jubilee in the following year. In the May preceding Jubilee Day, the Queen visited the East End to open the People's Palace. The route, seven miles long, was decorated in gay and characteristic style by the East Enders, and it was noticed that the Queen eyed the quaint, humorous devices with great pleasure, and at the opening ceremony at the Palace bowed and smiled at the references made to herself, in the speeches, in a delightfully informal manner. On the way back she visited the Lord Mayor at the Mansion House, and partook of tea and strawberries; this was the first time she had been at the Mansion House since she was the young Princess Victoria, and visited it with her mother. A boy in the crowd, when he found that the Queen had suddenly disappeared, asked eagerly, "Where is she gone?" "Gone?" replied an old basket woman. "Why, into the Lord Mayor's, to have a bite and a sup, poor thing, and I'll be bound as she needs it." The Queen has always shown a sympathetic interest in the East End, and one of her chaplains relates that after he had preached for the first time at Windsor he was summoned to her private apartment, and Her Majesty asked him a number of questions about East London and the state of labour at the docks, and then told him how she dealt with her cottagers at Balmoral, and about the schools she had established. "I could hardly realise," added this gentleman, "that I was talking with the Queen; she dismissed me filled with a vivid perception of her fine, royal courtesy, as well as her personal knowledge of and concern for the needy in her realm." In times of special distress in East London, the Queen has privately forwarded money for distribution. Another clergyman relates that when he was a boy in the Isle of Wight he saw the Queen coming out of a cottage where she had been to visit a sick person, and heard one workman say to another, "I like the Queen, Bill. I like having somebody to look up to"; and his companion replied, "Yes, and she is so good too."

There have been three royal jubilees in the history of this country, but not one in any way comparable to the jubilee of the 21st of June, 1887, when the whole land, together with the distant colonies and every quarter of the globe where the British flag waves, rang with the voice of jubilation that the great woman who had ennobled the crown was spared in health and strength to celebrate the fiftieth year of her reign. It was a thrilling moment when, in the blaze of the glorious June sunshine, the Queen drove out through the gates of Buckingham Palace on her way to Westminster Abbey, just as she had done fifty years before on her coronation day. But the bright young girl was now a grey-haired woman who had seen much sorrow and battled with many difficulties. Still, there was a gleam of triumph in her face, for were there not sons and daughters, grandchildren and great-grandchildren rising up to call her blessed, while the shouts of the multitudes which rent the air testified that throughout these fifty years she had retained the love and loyalty of her people? The scene in the Abbey was brilliant, as had been that earlier scene; but there was a hush of reverence over the assembly, for the monarch had come to publicly give thanks to Almighty God that she had been spared to see that day. At the end of the service the numerous members of her family were to personally offer their congratulations. The Lord Chamberlain had arranged it in correct style, but the Queen waived ceremony, and drawing each one in turn for a motherly embrace, turned the grand pageant into a happy family reunion. Fitting close, next day, to the festivities which had reigned everywhere throughout the country, was the monster school treat in Hyde Park, where thirty thousand school children of London were entertained. In the cool of the summer evening the Queen drove down the ranks and viewed the little ones; then the Prince of Wales brought to her carriage Florence Dunn, who had not missed an attendance at school for six years, and the Queen smiled down at the little champion, and, handing her the jubilee mug, said, "I am pleased to give you this memorial of my jubilee, dear child"; and this characteristic act closed the great celebration. It was an interesting coincidence that the minister of a country parish who had preached a sermon on the Queen's coronation also preached one on her jubilee; and still more wonderful was the case of an old lady in the town of Chipping Sodbury who had been present at George III.'s jubilee, and came out hale and hearty to help in the local celebration of Queen Victoria's, wearing the same bonnet, a Leghorn of coal-scuttle shape, which she had worn at the former jubilee.

After a few days' rest at Windsor, Her Majesty came to town again, and on the 30th of June opened the Holloway College for Women, thus testifying her interest in the advance of that higher education amongst women which, along with their improved legal and social status, has fittingly marked her reign. In the spring succeeding her jubilee, the Queen spent some weeks in Florence, always a favourite resort with her, as it had been with the Prince Consort. She was to be seen each morning, in the park adjacent to her villa, taking an airing in her donkey chair, and later in the day driving through the country districts, visiting the churches, and interesting herself in the life of the people. For one brief day she dropped her incognita and drove in public with her suite, and it seemed as though all Florence swarmed into the streets to greet her. The Queen did this to show her gratitude to the people for respecting her desire for privacy. She was fond of chatting with the country folk and one morning seeing two little girls gathering violets in a field near her villa, entered into conversation with them, and presented each of them with a jubilee sovereign, at which they rushed home to tell their mothers that the "Regina d'Inghilterra had given them a gilt medal with her likeness on it." On her way back from Florence the Queen visited her dying son-in-law, the Emperor Frederick, at Charlottenburg, a visit inexpressibly sad; but Her Majesty was not only able to comfort her daughter and cheer the dying Emperor — she acted as a peacemaker in the friction at Court caused by the Empress Frederick favouring the marriage of her daughter, Princess Victoria, with Prince Alexander of Battenberg. The Queen persuaded her daughter to drop the match, and by her tact brought about such a good understanding all round that Prince Bismarck, with whom she had a long interview, declared that "Her Majesty was gifted with a statesman-like wisdom of the highest order"; and indeed most political leaders who have come into personal contact with the Queen testify to her remarkable insight and sagacity.

Of late years her life has flowed on in the same steady, even course, with little jaunts to the Continent, visits to the Highlands, Christmas spent in good old English style at Osborne, and the discharge of occasional public Court functions in London; but wherever she may be her hand is at the helm, and telegraph and telephone messengers and despatch-boxes keep her hourly informed of everything which transpires even in the remotest part of her vast dominions. Her naturally robust constitution is preserved by the simplicity of her mode of life, spent largely in the open air, and her mind is kept bright and fresh by the interest she takes in the doings of the younger members of her extensive family circle. One hears much of Grand Old Men in these days; but who amongst them can say that he has been at his present post for sixty long years without one single day "off"? In all love and loyalty we would say that the Grand Old Woman upon the throne has "beaten the record." Her day is not done yet, therefore the time for a resume of her glorious reign has not arrived; but when the tale comes to be fully told, we know that there does not exist in the annals of this or any land a period so fraught with moral and material greatness as the reign of Victoria, Queen and Empress.

PERSONAL TASTES AND CHARACTERISTICS OF QUEEN VICTORIA

WHEN the women of Great Britain were subscribing their Jubilee gift to the Queen, a colony of Japanese women at Knightsbridge added their contributions with this characteristic wish: "Truly she must be a great 'Lady King'; may she live on an unshaken throne yet another fifty years, and after that the perpetual bliss!" Nearly ten years have rolled by since that memorable year of loyal enthusiasm, and our "Lady King" is with us still, venerated and beloved by all sections of the community at home and throughout her vast colonial dominions, as well as among the swarthy millions of India, who, though they have never seen her face, yet regard her as their Empress-Mother. She is honoured in the Courts of Europe as no English monarch has been before. It seems, indeed, that the Continent is rapidly coming under the sphere of British influence through the alliances made by the children, grandchildren, and great-grandchildren of Queen Victoria. When Russian ministers propose any course of procedure likely to upset the peace of Europe and bring England into the fray, the young Czar and Czarina promptly reply, "It must not be; we cannot have Grandmamma worried." The autocrat of all the Germans is not quite so considerate, perhaps; but if there is any one who can curb his impetuosity, and put the drag upon his ambition, it also is Grandmamma of England.

In America, where royalty is at a discount, and friction still shows itself in relations with the mother country, the influence of our "Lady King" is not unfelt American citizens still remember the hearty greetings which Queen Victoria sent to President Buchanan, forty years ago, along the lines of the newly laid Atlantic cable; such felicitations, however, were enough to make her grandfather, His Majesty King George III., turn in his grave. Neither can America forget the words of womanly sympathy and feeling which the Queen addressed to the wife of its murdered President, James Garfield. Upon that American citizen, the great philanthropist, George Peabody, she would gladly have conferred the Grand Cross of the Order of the Bath, but he declined all such honours. When asked what he would accept, he replied, "A letter from the Queen of England, which I may carry across the Atlantic and deposit as a memorial of one of her most faithful sons." It should be a bond of union between the two countries that in the Peabody Institute in the United States the miniature of Queen Victoria, which she sent to Mr. Peabody along with her letter, is deposited in a vault of famous relics side by side with a cane which belonged to Benjamin Franklin. It was owing to the tact of the Queen and Prince Consort in the wording of that famous despatch on the Trent affair, at the outbreak of the Civil War in America, that peace was preserved between England and the United States. Her Majesty has ever been more ready to try the power of moral suasion than of force, and only within the last year we have had an example of this in the autograph letters which the Queen addressed to the Sultan of Turkey regarding the atrocities in Armenia, and to her grandson of Germany upon his attitude to England over the rebellion and raid in the Transvaal.

Her Majesty has now sat upon the throne of this country for a longer period than any of her predecessors. The glories of the sixty years of her reign, and the unexampled prosperity which the country has enjoyed under her beneficent rule, are for the historian to tell; but when one pauses to study the personal character of the Queen, and the attributes which have made her beloved at home and revered abroad, they are to be summed up in one simple phrase — she is a good woman. Not faultless, certainly; the charming wilfulness of the child has a survival in maturer age. Strong and passionate in her attachments, the Queen could be, in her young days, quick and hasty even with those whom she loved best; but shallowness is no part of her nature, neither does she harbour resentment. Absolute truthfulness and sincerity are the qualities which dominate her character, and also gratitude towards those who have served her faithfully, be they great Ministers of State or humble servants. It is a part of the nobleness of her disposition that she does not assume that she has a right to special attention because of her high position. One frequently meets in her diaries with expressions of pleasure at kindness shown to her when visiting at the houses of her subjects, as though it were something unmerited. Among the many touching incidents of her gratitude to those who had been her faithful friends was the visit paid by her to Sir John Biddulph when he lay dying at Abergeldie Mains. "You have been very kind to me, your Majesty," said the dying man. "No," replied the Queen, as she pressed his hand, "it is you who have been very kind to me"

An utter detestation of shams is another of Her Majesty's characteristics, shown by the fact that those who have obtained her greatest confidence have been honest, even to bluntness. She likes to get at the root and reality of things, and the time-server stands no chance before her keen scrutiny. Her fondness for her faithful Highlanders has become almost a proverb, and she is never so happy as when talking with the old folks at Balmoral without form or ceremony, and much of her love for her Scottish home may be attributed to the fact that there she can throw off the restraints of royalty more thoroughly than in any other place. She is an exemplary landowner, and has erected schools, model cottages, established a free library, and provided a trained sick nurse for the tenants at Balmoral. To her cottagers at Osborne she is also ever the friend in time of need; and when she erected alms-houses on her estate for the use of poor old women, she retained one tiny room for herself, thus, as it were, becoming an alms-woman herself and keeping her poorer neighbours company. In matters of religion the Queen has shown herself singularly free from prejudice. At Balmoral she has always worshipped according to the simple style of the Scottish Church and partaken of its rites in communion, while she chose for her chief spiritual guides Dr. Norman Macleod and Principal Tulloch. In England the service in her private chapels is the simplest form of the Episcopalian Church, and her close friendship with Dean Stanley would point to the fact that she inclines to the broader school of thought, and thinks more of deeds than of creeds. She has ever set a good example in Sabbath observance; and many years ago, when it came to her knowledge that tradespeople were employed to bring provisions to Buckingham Palace on Sunday morning, she at once ordered that no eatables were to be brought into the Palace on Sunday.

The Queen is fond of quoting the saying of Schopenhauer, "If it were not for the honest faces of dogs, we should forget the very existence of sincerity"; and from her childhood to the present time she has always had dogs about her. Her earliest favourite, "Dash," a black-and-tan spaniel, was her constant companion when, as the Princess Victoria, she took her morning walk in Kensington Gardens, and his joyous bark was the first welcome she received on her return to Buckingham Palace from her coronation. "Looty," a lovely silken, long-haired dog brought by a British officer from China, was a later favourite. When the Summer Palace at Pekin was burning, this little dog was discovered curled up amongst soft shawls and rugs in one of the wardrobes, and the officer who rescued him and brought him to England as a present to the Queen gave him the significant name of "Looty." A picture of him by Mr. F. W Reyl was exhibited in the Royal Academy many years ago. Her Majesty has a special fondness for collies, and among these faithful animals "Noble" and

"Sharp" were for many years chief favourites, and always travelled with her to and from Balmoral. "'Noble,'" she writes in her diary, "is the most biddable dog I ever saw. He will hold a piece of cake in his mouth without eating it, until he may. If he thinks we are not pleased with him, he puts out his paws and begs in such an affectionate way." A beautiful collie named "Darnley II." has been for many years Her Majesty's chief pet. He has a special "cottage" of his own, apart from the kennels of the other dogs. In their beautiful homes in the grounds of Windsor Castle are to be seen skyes, collies, pugs, and dachs, in great variety; but the Queen's particular pride are her Italian "Spitzes," a breed of beautiful buff-coloured dogs which she was the first to introduce into this country. "Marco," with his lovely white coat and almost human intelligence, is another chief favourite with his royal mistress. It would be a mistake to suppose that these pets are unduly pampered, for the Queen believes that plain living induces high thinking in dogs as well as in human beings.

Her Majesty has been one of the most accomplished horsewomen of her time, and her ponies have an almost equal share of attention with her dogs. There is "Jessie," which was her favourite riding mare for twenty-five years, and carried her through many a Highland expedition; then there are her two Shetland ponies, and "Flora" and "Alma," presented by King Victor Emmanuel, and a grey Arab, a present from the Thakore of Morvi. The royal mews at Windsor cover an extent of four acres, and have accommodation for one hundred horses. The harness-horses are nearly all of them grey, and those for the broughams are dark chestnut. But specially proud is the Queen of her twelve cream-coloured horses, which I have been privileged to see in the mews at Buckingham Palace, looking very beautiful indeed with their long, silky tails nearly touching the ground. Their ancestors took the girl Queen, nearly sixty years ago, to her coronation, and the stock is always kept up for Her Majesty's use on State occasions.

An amusing little favourite of the Queen was "Picco," which she used to drive in a pony-carriage some years ago. He was a Sardinian pony, presented by the King of that country, and was only forty-four inches high. That charming naturalist Frank Buckland has given an amusing account of his attempts to sketch this fussy, nervous little fellow, who was highly indignant at having his measurements taken. The Queen was greatly diverted by the account of her pet's behaviour, for she is fond of studying the characters of the animals about her, and likes them to have their pictures taken. Bushey Park is used as a kind of home of rest for the pet horses who are no longer fit for active service. There "Picco" was sent to end his days, and, as a useful lesson in humility, he had "Alderney," a costermonger's rescued victim, given him for a companion. One day, when the Queen was driving in the Isle of Wight, she saw a costermonger savagely beating a beautiful white pony, and, stopping her carriage, she offered to buy the ill-used animal, in order to save him from his life of misery. She gave him the name of "Alderney," and promoted him to a life of ease in Bushey Park, where he doubtless entertained his aristocratic friend "Picco" with the doings of costerland. To-day the Queen's chief favourite is "Jacquot," the strong, handsome donkey with the white nose and knotted tail, which draws her chair in the gardens of Frogmore or through the shady glades at Osborne, and has accompanied Her Majesty to the Highlands and to Florence and the Riviera.

The Queen's love for the brute creation does not limit itself to those animals who have the good fortune to be her pets. She has been a warm supporter of those societies which labour to ameliorate the sufferings of animals, and views the modern thirst for scientific discovery by means of vivisection with apprehension. In a letter sent at her command by Sir Thomas Biddulph, in 1872, to Lord Harrowby, then President of the Society for the Prevention of Cruelty to Animals, this passage occurs: "The Queen hears and reads with horror of the sufferings which the brute creation often undergo from the thoughtlessness of the ignorant, and, she fears, also, sometimes from experiments in the pursuit of science. For the removal of the former the Queen trusts much to the progress of education, and, in regard to the pursuit of science, she hopes that the entire advantage of those anaesthetic discoveries from which man has derived so much benefit himself in the alleviation of suffering may be freely extended to the lower animals." Her Majesty is a great sympathiser with that branch of the Society's work which aims at educating the children in the board schools to a sense of kindness to dumb animals by means of prizes given for essays upon the subject.

The Queen's anxiety to protect lambs from what she conceived to be premature killing resulted in rather an amusing fiasco some years ago. She had been reading gloomy articles in the newspapers about the decrease of English sheep, and she immediately attributed it to the excessive slaughter of very young lambs, and gave orders that no lamb was to be used in the royal household. The price of the meat at once fell to four-pence a pound, and it became necessary to explain to the Queen that the consumption of lamb was not the cause of the trouble, it was a question of breeding, and she then withdrew her mandate. This little incident is but one of many which serve to show her anxiety to promote the public good by her example. Many years ago, before county councils existed for the supervision of public amusements, the Queen made her influence felt in Birmingham. At a fete in Aston Park a woman who had been forced to walk on a rotten tight-rope was dashed to pieces in a shocking manner.

Such was the callousness of the committee that they permitted the festivities to proceed in spite of the dreadful occurrence. A few days later the Mayor of Birmingham was the astonished recipient of a letter from the Queen's Secretary, to this effect: "Her Majesty cannot refrain from making known her personal feelings of horror that one of her subjects — a female — should have been sacrificed to the gratification of the demoralising taste, unfortunately prevalent, for exhibitions attended with the greatest danger to the performers. If any proof were wanting that such exhibitions are demoralising, it would be found in the decision arrived at to continue the festivities, the hilarity, and the sports of the occasion after an event so melancholy. The Queen trusts that the Mayor, in common with the townspeople of Birmingham, will use his influence to prevent in future the degradation by such exhibitions of the park which she and the beloved Prince Consort opened for the rational recreation of the people."

In the early days of railway travelling the Queen, who, with characteristic fearlessness, had been one of the first to trust to the "steam demon," was very active in bringing pressure to bear upon the railway companies to induce them to take greater precaution for the protection of passengers. It was she who, in conjunction with the Prince Consort, put an end in this country to the barbarous custom of duelling. Recently, when standing on Wimbledon Common looking at the spot where the last duel in this country was fought, an old man came up to me who had himself been a witness of the scene, and he described it in quaint and graphic language. "I shall never forget," he said, "my feelings as a lad when I saw the man who had been shot lying with his dead, upturned face upon the turf, and Lord Cardigan, who had shot him, hurrying away with his friends. Ah, well! the Queen put an end to that sort of thing; she's done a few good things in the course of her time."

To-day, now that legislation has become so much more humanitarian in its scope than it was forty or fifty years ago, one is apt to lose sight of the immense influence of royal example. In the good old days the chief restraint on social customs was fashion. As was the Court, so were the people. Probably no English monarch has done more for the purification of society and for the elevation of a simple domestic life than Victoria. If great ladies to-day prefer to spend their leisure hours in the support of pet philanthropies instead of the excitement of lotteries, was it not the Queen who set the vogue by associating her great name with schemes of beneficence? She was a visitor in the wards of our great hospitals long before ladies of birth and social position took up such work to any extent. That philanthropy is to-day fashionable is due to a wave of influence coming from the throne and permeating all classes of society. All the Queen's daughters, and indeed daughters-in-law also, are women who delight in good works; and although they owe much of their impetus in that direction to the Prince Consort, it was the Queen who gave her children such an admirable father. Her Majesty chose her husband for his good qualities, and nothing but her sanction and support made it possible for him to carry through his schemes. The nation was at one time barely respectful to him, and did not awaken to a full appreciation of his merits until it was too late. But for the Queen, Prince Albert might have occupied no better a position in the country than did the insignificant husband of Queen Anne.

Another of Her Majesty's characteristics which has influenced the national life of her own sex is the Queen's love of fresh air and outdoor exercise. There is a connection between our venerated sovereign taking her breakfast in a tent on the lawn and spending many hours of each day driving, whatever the weather may be, and the fine, healthy, well-developed girl of the period swinging her tennis racket, playing hockey, and boating and cycling. When the Queen was young such things were not, and the mammas of that time were probably shocked when they first heard, fifty and more years ago, of Her Majesty going deer-stalking with her husband for nine hours at a stretch, undertaking perilous mountain expeditions, and walking about in the wilds of Balmoral with a hood drawn over her bonnet to protect her face from the rain. She was fond, too, of taking an early walk before breakfast; and on one occasion, when paying a visit to Blair Athole, she set out alone early one morning before any one was about, and wandered so far — beguiled by the fresh autumn air — that she lost her way, and was obliged to appeal to some reapers whom she saw working in a field to show her the way back. She always encouraged her daughters to take plenty of outdoor exercise, and they were expert skaters at a time when the pastime was an uncommon one for ladies. Princess Alice was a particularly graceful skater, and after her marriage found that she was nearly the only lady in Darmstadt who could skate.

The Queen gave her countenance to ladies riding the tricycle at a very early stage of the introduction of that machine. It was while taking her favourite drive along the Newport Road in the Isle of Wight that she for the first time saw a lady riding a tricycle, and she was so much pleased that she ordered two machines to be sent to Osborne for some of her ladies to learn to ride upon. When the more expeditious bicycle came into use, Her Majesty looked askance for a time at ladies using it; but now she takes the greatest delight in watching the merry cycling parties of princesses which start daily from Balmoral in the autumn, and she has enjoyed many of her hearty laughs at those who were in the learner's stage, and had not mastered the mystery of maintaining the balance. That latest innovation in the way of vehicles — the motor-car — is regarded by the Queen with special interest, for when she was a girl there was an effort made to introduce coaches run by steam on to the roads, but the public did not take to the idea of these horseless carriages, and so they dropped out of existence, and "Jarvey" won the day. On at least one occasion Her Majesty rode in one: it was when she was about twelve years of age. With her mother, the Duchess of Kent, she had been to visit His Majesty King George IV. at the Royal Lodge, and they made the return journey from Windsor to London in a steam coach. There is an old man still living at Windsor who is not a little proud that he can recall the occasion.

In her attitude to modern inventions the Queen has hitherto shown herself ready to accept new ideas, but it is said that she does not take to the electric light, and will not have it introduced into the royal palaces. At Balmoral she has the rooms lighted by candles, and burns wood fires, as she finds this old-fashioned style cosier, and it reminds her of her young days. The Queen first adopted gas in 1854, when it was used to light the new ball-room at Buckingham Palace on the occasion of the first visit of Napoleon and the Empress Eugenie to this country. The ceiling of the room was decorated in various colours to enable Her Majesty to form an idea of the effect of the new illuminant. She and the Prince Consort were so pleased with it that they shortly afterwards introduced it into Windsor Castle. Probably the Queen thinks that to have witnessed one entire revolution in the way of domestic lighting is enough in a lifetime, and she will leave the adoption of the electric light to younger people.

The early British custom of erecting cairns, or heaps of stones, to commemorate events is one greatly in favour with the Queen. The first royal cairn was erected when she took possession of Balmoral, and the estate is now quite rich in these unique memorials, there being one to commemorate the Prince Consort's death and the marriages of each of her children. One might say that Her Majesty has a passion for having memorials of her domestic joys and sorrows, and she is most punctilious in the observance of anniversaries. She keeps her own birthday, and has a birthday cake like other people, and is keenly appreciative of the presents which are sent to her by every member of her family, even to the youngest branches. The Prince Consort's birthday is also observed, and his health drunk in silence.

Since her great bereavement her mind has naturally dwelt much on death observances, and she has herself drawn up a complete code of directions for the arrangement of royal funerals and layings out. Different shrouds are directed to be used for the male and female members of the family, also for the married and unmarried; and female members of the royal family abroad are to be represented by one of their own sex. When the Duchess of Cambridge died in 1889, the Queen insisted that the funeral should be in semi-State, although the aged Duchess had herself desired to be buried quite privately. She was one of the few left who had known the Queen in the heyday of her youth and had really loved and cared for her, and Her Majesty was determined that her much-revered aunt should be buried with the observances due to her high birth as well as to her excellent character. The apartments used by deceased royalties in the Queen's palaces and houses are kept locked up. Those of Princess Charlotte at Claremont have been preserved as she left them for more than seventy years. Prince Albert's private rooms at Windsor, Osborne, and Balmoral, and the Duchess of Kent's at Frogmore, also remain undisturbed, and the Queen has testified her special esteem for John Brown by directing that the rooms which he used at Windsor Castle are to be kept sacred to his memory. Her Majesty has a great objection to embalming, and has prohibited it with regard to royal persons, unless the circumstances are very exceptional. After the sad death of the Prince Imperial at the hands of the Zulus, and the impossibility there was of preserving his body for the Empress to take a last look at it, the Queen so far relaxed her regulations as to permit the various accessories for embalming being taken out when one of the royal family undertook foreign service. The wisdom of this arrangement has been sadly seen in the case of Prince Henry of Battenberg.

Her Majesty is a little behind the spirit of the times in regard to regulations for mourning. She advocates absolute retirement for a time in the case of bereaved people, and the most lugubrious signs of outward mourning. It would seem, also, that she does not favour the re-marriage of widows, judging from the significant fact that not one of the royal widows, be she young or be she middle-aged, has been provided with a second husband. In the case of widowers Her Majesty's strictures are not so severe.

She has instituted several changes with regard to royal weddings. She herself set the example of being married in the morning, royal marriages having formerly been celebrated in an evening. It was not customary in former reigns for royalties to retire for a honeymoon; His Majesty King George III. remained at St. James's and held levees immediately after his marriage. The Queen and Prince Albert had a brief honeymoon of two days at Windsor; then the Duchess of Kent and all the Court came flocking down to escort the royal pair back to a round of functions and festivities in London. Even that very young bride the Princess Royal had, like her mother, only two days of absolute retirement. Since that the royal honeymoons have been gradually increasing in length, and the latest bride, Princess Maud, has had a whole week of seclusion, and then it was only broken in upon by a visit from her mother and sister. The custom of brides mingling myrtle with their orange blossoms is, as we all know, a fashion introduced by the Queen.

In matters of Court etiquette Her Majesty is punctilious to a degree, and her memory for pedigrees, as for faces, is unrivalled. A story is told by a Court lady that a question arose at the royal table between herself and Lord Beaconsfield as to the genealogy of some obscure Italian duke who had suddenly come into notice. No one could tell who he was. "There is one person who could give the information," said Lord Beaconsfield, "and that is the Queen." He took the first opportunity of asking the question. "The Duca di —?" replied Her Majesty. "Oh yes, I remember perfectly," and she forthwith gave a full history of his family. Prime Ministers of modern times have sometimes found the Queen's remarkable memory a little embarrassing, as in discussion on political questions she will confront them with the views of Peel or Palmerston, or with the advice given her by Lord Melbourne in the first year of her reign; and it is reported that Lord Salisbury was once driven to delicately hint that there was a difference between the state of affairs in '37 and '87.

Her Majesty has always been very strict with regard to regulations for Court dress. All ladies, of whatever age, are required to appear in bodices with low necks and short sleeves. Plumes must always be worn standing erect from the back of the head; no modification is permitted. When a lady who formerly reigned as a society beauty and is now a theatrical star was to be presented, she arranged her Court head-dress in quite an artistic manner, pinning down the feathers upon her lovely hair in a most becoming manner. All went well until she passed before the Court functionary preparatory to making the entree; then she was ordered to remove the pins, as no lady was permitted to enter the Presence except with her plumes erect.

It had always been the practice to forbid the attendance at drawing-rooms of ladies divorced, even though it was for no fault of their own; but the Queen, with her admirable sense of justice, came to the conclusion that this was scarcely fair, and decided that a lady of blameless life ought not to be excluded from Court by reason of her husband's misdeeds. The matter was brought before the Cabinet some years ago, but allowed to drop without its being decided. The question was revived in 1889, and it was arranged that ladies debarred by divorce may make special application for admission to Court to the Queen herself, who decides on the merit of each case, after having had the report of the trial laid before her. There is, I believe, a record of one lady who had obtained divorces from two husbands in succession gaining the Queen's permission to be presented on her third marriage.

To one so fond of outdoor life and the beauties of nature as Her Majesty, flowers are naturally a special delight, and she prefers to see them growing rather than when used for indoor decoration. In the grounds at Osborne there is a flower-bed specially planted for the Queen's pleasure with pinks and carnations, as she is very fond of these old-fashioned flowers, and frequently takes tea on a spot near to the bed. During her drives from Osborne to Newport she had noticed the lovely gardens and houses belonging to Mr. Nunn, the famous manufacturer of the lace called by his name, and one day expressed a wish to see over them. Ever afterwards a basket of Mr. Nunn's choicest blooms was sent daily to the Queen when she was at Osborne, and the gift gave her the greatest pleasure. At the time of the Jubilee a loyal gentleman suggested the wearing of the Queen's favourite flower as a badge, and wrote to Sir Henry Ponsonby to inquire what it was. Her Majesty replied that in summer she perferred the rose to any other flower. Probably it is the sweet and delicate odour of the national flower as well as its beauty which pleases the Queen, as she greatly dislikes strong perfumes.

Speaking of scents, one is reminded that Her Majesty had such a dislike to the smell of cigars and tobacco that smoking was for many years prohibited in Windsor Castle, a restriction in which the Prince Consort fully concurred. Cards requesting that gentlemen would not smoke were neatly framed and hung in the rooms of the lords-in-waiting and equerries of the royal suite, and the servants and workpeople were forbidden to smoke inside the Castle. No such rigid restriction exists to-day, which is attributed to the influence of John Brown, who liked his pipe, and, being as canny as he was faithful, persuaded the Queen that a little tobacco smoke was "no a bad thing to have about a hoose."

Previous to the death of the Prince Consort the Queen was devoted to music, and spent a great deal of time both in singing and playing. They were both most anxious to see music more universal in the homes of the people, and strongly advocated its being taught in the public schools — a fact which may be interesting to those engaged in controversy to-day regarding the use of pianos in the board schools. Since the death of the Prince she has scarcely played at all, but she remains to the present time one of the kindest patrons of singers and musicians, who count a command to perform before the Queen a personal pleasure, as she is so appreciative, and will talk with them of the great "stars" whom she has listened to in the days gone by Sketching was the Queen's favourite recreation as a child, and so it remains to-day. She is particularly proud of her art collection at Windsor, and, when there, does not let many weeks go by without taking a look round the Royal Library, which contains one of the finest collections of engravings and specimens of old masters, both English and foreign. But her unrivalled collection of miniatures is her particular pride, and she boasts sometimes that she had but one rival in the country, and that was his Scottish majesty, the late Duke of Buccleuch.

The Queen will live in history as the most enlightened and consistent of constitutional monarchs, as well as being revered as a great and noble woman. Those who have been privileged to enjoy her friendship all speak of the beautiful blending of naivete and kindness with great personal dignity which render her so charming in private life. As a ruler she is wise, judicious and sagacious, and above everything distinguished by a high sense of duty. Reverence deep and lasting lives for her in the hearts of the people, and in concluding this story of her personal life one can but echo those beautiful lines of Mrs. Crosland:

"Victoria! writ large in lines of light,
The name through coming ages will remain
In foremost rank with those great few that blight
Ne'er tarnished, shining on without a stain."

Printed in Great Britain
by Amazon